MW01196195

# Soul-less Society

## The Ultimate Deception
## That Took The Land of Plenty
## to A Nation of Death

ANGELINE MARIE

DEFIANCE PRESS
& PUBLISHING

Soul-less Society: The Ultimate Deception That Took The Land of Plenty to A Nation of Death

ISBN-13: 978-1-959677-78-9 (Paperback)
ISBN-13: 978-1-959677-77-2 (eBook)

Published by Defiance Press and Publishing, LLC

Bulk orders of this book may be obtained by contacting Defiance Press and Publishing, LLC. www.defiancepress.com.

Public Relations Dept. – Defiance Press & Publishing, LLC
281-581-9300
pr@defiancepress.com

Defiance Press & Publishing, LLC
281-581-9300
2685 S. Loop 336W Suite B
Conroe, TX 77304
info@defiancepress.com

www.TruthSeekersRadioShow.com

# Dedication

I would like to dedicate this book to our Lord Jesus Christ—it is a message He put on my heart to disseminate internationally.

Thank you to my husband, family, and friends for always encouraging me while I worked on this project. Thank you to my sister in Christ, Jill Caballero, for always pushing me to do better.

Thank you to the late Dr. Stan Monteith for inspiring me to start *The Truth Seekers Radio Show*. Thank you to Tom Donahue for mentoring me after I started the radio show.

In memory of my late Uncle Joe who is now in heaven and left this earth with the final words, "Praise God!"

And finally, to all of the Truth Seekers around the world!

*"I have no greater joy than to hear that my children walk in truth."*
3 John 1:4.

# Foreword

*And he causeth all, both small and great, rich and poor, free and bond, to receive a mark in their right hand, or in their foreheads:*

*And that no man might buy or sell, save he that had the mark, or the name of the beast, or the number of his name.*

*Here is wisdom. Let him that hath understanding count the number of the beast: for it is the number of a man; and his number is six hundred three-score and six.*

Revelation 13:16-18 (KJV)

Anyone who understands the foregoing recitations will know exactly where the United States of America is headed, despite all of the rantings of politicians and pundits about how things will "change" if they're elected.

Understandably, what you'll discover in this masterful work is the lead-up to the great event and what is to become of those who do not kowtow to "the Beast".

There are so many interpretations of these passages, as much as historians have attempted to interpret the chronological perspectives the author posits in this work, albeit not as succinctly as Angeline Marie explores them.

Those of little faith have fulfilled the Scriptures' telling apostasy, the falling away, to the extreme, by allowing the United States government to lead them into certain doom through all of the Hegelian mechanisms portrayed in this book.

The author of this introduction, who has committed the greater portion of his lifespan into the Word and the Law, understands the concepts explained throughout *Soul-less Society*, as anyone who has the wisdom and knowledge to see, hear and understand what is going on around them will see the destiny of this once great nation and what is to become of its people.

The marks of freedom and prosperity that have been instituted by our forefathers have been gradually whittled away and left us all like frogs in warm water that has been slowly increased to a boil. If the above Biblical text is true, then our outcome may be unavoidable, but not without the hope of salvation.

It is implied that forward thinking by everyone who carefully examines the testimony in this book will understand that this is not their world and not one reader bargained for this outcome. However, anyone who can come to the understanding of why and how the downfall of America was allowed to happen can first take stock in its Constitution. Our Founding Fathers put their faith in God, the Father of our Lord Jesus Christ when drafting it. The historical perspectives shown in this work reflect those same tenets, which expose corruptness and evil, manifesting fully and exposing those who sought to "dilute" America from what She was destined to become, into a "babylon" of sorts, much to the chagrin of those who have no hope and have given up on such destinies.

Do not give up the faith. Pray without ceasing. Take action where things matter most. Do not disregard your family and your community. Understand that God is first in all things. Understand that your family is second and your country is third, as dismal as it may seem. Ours is to have a *glass half full* if it must come to that, not as others whose glass is half empty, whose "scales" remain over their eyes and cannot see what you see.

I would not have posited the text of Revelation within the Foreword of this book, if its reader lacked "the understanding" as described in the last verse of St. John the Divine. It was meant to enlighten and open your mind to what you are about to read and absorb within the covers of this work. God's Blessings to you as you further your knowledge of what matters as to the complacency of those throughout time, who have ignored the difference between good and evil and that the "outcome"… collectively … of our future … is inevitable.

Dave Krieger
Author of *Clouded Titles*
Radio Talk Show Host of The Power Hour

# Preface

How did such a strong and leading country, the United States of America, go from being a prosperous nation with moral people, a land of plenty, to being such a declining and morally bankrupt nation that promotes depravity, death, and its own destruction, a nation of death, in a relatively short span of time?

My immediate thought is that the majority of the time I notice that people of spiritual faith, in particular Christians, seem to embrace political conservatism or a more traditional perspective, and people who tend to be atheist, agnostic, or Christian liberal, tend to lean left politically with a more progressive perspective. I am not saying this is always the case; I am saying this is generally the case.

Why? What seems to be the catalyst for this? Why does it matter?

It was at that moment that I realized, try as hard as you may, you cannot separate politics and religion. What do I mean by this? In our human nature—they go together. Our spiritual principles, whether religious or nonreligious (i.e., atheist, agnostic, etc.) are the very foundation of our political beliefs—they are not separate.

Society has taught us that it is taboo to discuss politics and religion;

when the two are inseparable, why is this?

I contend that we need to discuss politics and religion if we want to answer the question of how the United States went from being a land of plenty to being a nation of death because they go hand in hand. Notice I did not say we need to agree or convince each other of our political or religious convictions, but just that we should, in a free country, feel comfortable discussing these subjects in public, with family, friends, co-workers, etc.

Instead, the media has propagandized us into thinking that these subjects are too taboo—off-limits—to discuss outside our inner circles. What are they afraid of? I think those in media and those in control are afraid we may discover a truth that they have been hiding from us. They usually seem to label ideas that are counter to mainstream narratives as conspiracy theories or ridiculous ideas. If these ideas are so outlandish, why do they care if we discuss them? Could it be because there may be some truth to these ideas?

In my opinion, this is nothing more than a tactic to get people to "self-censor" so they don't spread their ideas—because they may actually take hold.

This, in turn, divides people, rather than uniting them, and that, my friends is the underlying agenda of the globalists, the elite, those in control.

For over 240 years, the American people have for the most part enjoyed a certain amount of civility and prosperity in a free society. I am not saying there have been no bumps along the way. In my opinion, there is an operation underway to deliberately throw the United States and the nations of the world off the rails spiritually to cause the chaos the world is experiencing today. Why? To usher in a new age of globalism, complete control over everyone and everything, by a few at the top. This is the physical manifestation of an underlying spiritual war.

For the global agenda to gain steam, its proponents need to put a wedge between people or groups of people to keep them from uniting. This is the only way to drive their agenda forward. What is their agenda? While I will mention the agendas in their physical form, I will primarily emphasize their spiritual foundation in this book.

I will not hide my personal convictions. My worldview comes from a traditional conservative, Christian slant. This means that I believe more is going on in the fight than what you can see.

This fight carries to a whole other level. In the physical world, it plays out as the globalists vs. the non-globalists, the governments vs. the people, one race or group against another race or group—but the ultimate fight is in the spiritual realm. It boils down to GOOD (God) vs. EVIL (devil). God's name is in the word *good* and the devil's name encapsulates *evil*.

I wrote this book because I wanted to unveil the spiritual variable of the equation; to show the connection to the physical chaos we live through daily, and to encourage you to sift through the media rubbish we hear every day.

No matter what you believe, I sincerely hope to encourage you to think beyond what you are told to think on a daily basis, to become a free thinker, a seeker of the truth—the absolute truth.

Then you will be able to answer the question of how the land of plenty became a nation of death and how you can help change it!

# Contents

# Chapter 1

# How Do You Know What You Know?

Our nation is collapsing around us. Every day we witness another piece of our society being destroyed.

Pick your poison—spiritual degradation, government corruption, corporate fascism, failing healthcare and education systems, a compromised media, environmental degradation and manipulation, violence, rising crime. The list is endless.

Which is most important? Where does one start in terms of addressing these escalating problems?

When it was placed on my heart to write this book, I decided the most important consequence of these world problems is death—the death of people around the world. I had to write the message that, although one can never escape physical death, there is hope that we can escape an eternal spiritual death. We can escape the trajectory we are on. It is never too late to accept the gift of eternal life. We've watched the land of plenty move toward a nation of death—but take heart; there is hope.

We read in John 5:24, "Verily, verily, I say unto you, He that heareth my word, and believeth on him that sent me, hath everlasting life, and shall not come into condemnation, but is passed from death unto life."

## The Awakening!

In January 2000, I landed a job with a doctor-owned software company that was developing an electronic medical records program. My job was to test the software and deliberately try to break it or find the faults or "bugs" before its release.

We were a small group that included a couple of programmers, a database engineer, and quality testers. After a couple of months working at this company, I became very bored. I told the owner my dilemma and gave him my two weeks' notice. He asked if I would stay on until he found someone else since they faced a deadline for the first release. I told him I would agree to stay temporarily.

Since our office was small and the work was tedious at times, the owner allowed the employees to listen to Internet radio with headphones. This was when, out of boredom, I stumbled onto a radio network called, Liberty Works Radio Network, led by the late John B. Kotmair, Jr. I also found a radio program called *Radio Liberty* with host Dr. Stan Monteith.

At the time, I was thirty-six years-old, and I didn't follow politics. I suppose I was too busy working and trying to figure out my life's purpose—and there it was—my first lessons via the Internet. I remember hearing about the globalist elite and their plan to take America down. Our middle class was the problem. If the American people were prosperous, the globalist plan for a New World Order (carried out through the United Nations) could not come to fruition. It sounded like a bad movie.

When I was in college studying journalism, I saw glimpses of this takedown, but the picture did not become crystal clear until I learned certain things at my software job. When I was a journalism student, I thought there was a spiritual war between good and evil—and this is true—it is the foundation of the takedown. However, what I did not know until I heard Dr. Stan Monteith's broadcasts was that the globalists were using American institutions to brainwash and carry out their plans in the physical world.

I remember thinking, *How could the United States government go against its own citizens in such evil and insidious ways?* Answer: Because a spiritual war is manifesting and being carried out by political and ideological means in the physical realm.

This is what it is all about. It didn't take long for me to learn that there were sellouts on both sides of the political spectrum—whether Republican or Democrat.

I realized that the Lord had kept me at this tedious software job for a much bigger purpose—the purpose I was looking for—to learn so that one day He could use my life in bigger ways than I could imagine. And the irony is that at age thirty-six, even though I was a lifelong Christian and had a journalism degree, I felt empty regarding my life's calling. I knew there had to be more, and I wanted to know what is was.

## The Calling that Was "Not" to Be!

When I was in my early twenties, I was a journalism and communications major. I wanted to be the next Deborah Norville on NBC's *Today Show*. I was a reporter and anchor for our college news show for a couple of semesters. Every week or so, we would have to think of story ideas based on campus life. Someone suggested I interview and do a story on a Christian students' group on campus. Who were they? What did they do? Why? I thought it was a good idea. I didn't even know they existed until someone suggested their group as a story topic.

I called the president of the group thinking he'd probably be glad to do an interview with me to get exposure for the group. Instead I was shocked when his reaction was very guarded, even negative. He confided in me that he was very hesitant to do an interview because the last time he did one for the college, it had a very negative slant about the group. I told him I would be objective and that I would never purposely slant a story.

Eventually, I gained his confidence, and he agreed to an interview. I showed up to the interview accompanied by a student photographer. It went well and was an objective story about the group. We completed the interview, and the photographer and I were on our way.

At the time, an assistant teacher was in charge of the television production studio. We would turn our video, audio voiceovers, and scripts over to him for editing.

The day arrived for my story to air. We produced the news programs 'live-on-tape,' meaning they were shot and recorded in real time as if live, but were broadcast at a later time on a public access channel. This meant my story package aired within the program, and as far as the director was concerned, there would be no chance to edit or change the content—it was *in the can*, a done deal.

As I sat at the news desk watching my story air, I would have liked to crawl under the table. My story ran as another negative piece on the Christian college group. I was shocked and embarrassed. The editor had strategically edited my news story as a negative shot at the group whose trust I had worked so hard to gain.

At that moment, I learned two things:

1. The communist propaganda that my journalism and ethics professors taught was rampant in other countries, was alive and well in my own supposed free country.

2. The teaching assistant who edited my news story had a definite agenda against the Christian group and used my story to carry it out.

At the time, I realized if this was how the media behaved on a college campus, it was probably even worse in the real world. Since this scenario took place, I have been critical of the media. Their role, as I was taught in my journalism and ethics classes, was to be the watchdog of government for the people.

Unfortunately, most mainstream news outlets and journalists, in my opinion, are high-profile, well-paid prostitutes that are the lapdogs of the government and are given the task to manufacture and push out propaganda—exactly like the communist journalists I learned about years ago.

Many decades have passed since I learned these lessons. I have continued to study and learn about the propaganda assault that the American people have been under for a long time.

I spoke earlier about trying to find my life's purpose. I have been fortunate enough to work on several media projects so that I could use my journalism and media production skills.

In 2012, I started to host and produce *The Truth Seekers Radio Show*. In 2017, I felt the Lord leading me to launch the K-Star Talk Radio Network and in 2022 the Kingdom Star Radio Network. In 2020, I did some short reports for *The Tom Donahue Show*—and now this book.

When I was in college, I had planned to be successful in mainstream journalism. I am happy to report that I failed miserably because God knows best, and He sent me down a different road. Only time will tell where it leads me.

I told this story so that you understand my perspective when I present ideas and observations throughout this book.

Our beliefs are the sum of our experiences in this world. What we think we know and believe as individuals is based on our personal history from the day we are born.

## How Do You Know What You Know?

*Stop* and clear your mind.

Think about everything you know. Where did you learn what you know?

Chances are you learned from your family, friends, teachers, pastors, other people in your life, all forms of media (TV, movies, music, encyclopedias, radio, etc.), government, educational systems, NASA, scientists, doctors, political figures, religious leaders, sports figures, celebrities—to name a few sources. And where did these sources learn what they *think* they know?

In most of these cases, you have believed what these sources told you is the *truth* based on your *faith* in the sources themselves—*not* based on *proof* or verification that you saw, touched, smelled, or experienced firsthand.

Try to stay with me on this.

As a child, you attend school and are told what to believe—and you do. In some cases, you are told some of these beliefs are based on scientific proof ... and some may be, but not all.

When was the last time you *actually carried out a study to prove a theory* you were told was a fact?

In school, you are taught a particular lesson and told it is a fact. You are not told that what you are being taught may have been funded and produced by an educational or scientific establishment entity that has a vested interest in a particular outcome backing a specific agenda.

Teachers and thought leaders conveniently leave out this part. Why? Simply put, if you knew that the lesson was funded by a particular entity with an already established agenda, you may not believe in the outcome or belief they want you to accept as fact.

Some things you learn in school are not debatable; they are fact. In mathematics, 2+1=3. This is not up for debate, although the New Math advocates will try to convince you that 2+1 can equal anything you decide.

The point is that some of the information you were taught in school, such as the mathematical equation above, is a fact that can be proven simply by counting out the numbers being added together. On the flip side, you were taught other lessons you were told were fact, when in reality they were only theories.

In my opinion, one of these theories is evolution. This is why they call it the theory of evolution—because scientists who want to embrace this theory cannot prove it to be an absolute truth.

In spite of the fact that evolution cannot be proven as an absolute truth, the public education system in the United States presents evolution as a proven fact. The question is: While evolution is only a theory, "Why do some people believe it is a proven fact?"

I contend it is because as young students, we are made to believe that the higher authorities, in this case, teachers, professors, scientists, government, educational systems, are teaching facts when in reality they may not be facts. Teachers may be teaching theories with an agenda that is paid for by a small group. People have paid for students to be taught a certain agenda which is emphasized as fact.

Others believe in creationism—that men were created in the image of God. Why is this not taught as well? While evolution cannot be proven—how is it that evolution has become the primary theory taught in U.S. schools?

## Theories Taught as Fact in U.S. Schools

Most young people today would be shocked to know that at one time the U.S. public school system taught creationism as the origin of life. So how did it change from creationism to evolution?

The leading narrative for the origin of life changed based on whoever was in leadership roles at any particular time in history. Whoever holds the power sets the belief of the day.

While a majority of the people in the U.S believed in creationism before the introduction of Darwinism in 1859, now many have come to accept evolution as the dominant theory.

The most recent theory related to the origin of life is "intelligent design." Some beliefs circulating within the intelligent design camp claim the possibility that mankind was created from other outside intelligent beings—such as an alien race.

As ridiculous as this may sound to a majority of people, most notably the creationists, if the public school systems started to teach this as a dominant origin of life theory for the next generation—within twenty years, it would not only be accepted, but deeply ingrained in society's consciousness as the new absolute truth.

Here are other examples of unproven theories that have been accepted as absolute truth.

If you've attended an educational institution anywhere in the world, you've probably heard of Sir Isaac Newton's law of gravitation. We have been taught this as fact and as shown in David Wardlaw Scott's book, published in 1901, *Terra Firma: The Earth Not a Planet, Proved from Scripture, Reason, and Fact*, even Newton himself did not profess his law of gravitation as anything other than hypothesis.

"Sir Isaac Newton himself does not even attempt to give one proof of the truth of Gravitation; with him it is only supposition from beginning to end. Thus he says, ... 'But the reason these properties of gravity I could never hitherto deduce from phenomena; and am unwilling to frame hypotheses about them; for whatever is not deduced from phenomena ought to be called an hypothesis, and no sort of hypotheses are allowable in experimental philosophy wherein propositions are deduced from phenomena, and not made general by deduction.'"[1]

Yet the educational system has introduced Newton's gravitation theory as a fact rather than a possibility; I believe this is how the educational systems slowly take over the minds of men.

In the same book, Scott demonstrates the conclusions he arrives at when he exercises independent, critical thinking skills regarding the law of gravitation.

> I remember being taught when a boy, that the Earth was a great ball, revolving at a very rapid rate around the Sun, and, when I expressed to my teacher my fears that the waters of the oceans would tumble off, I was told that they were prevented from doing so by Newton's great Law of Gravitation, which kept everything in its proper place. I presume that my countenance must have shown some signs of incredulity, for my teacher immediately added—I can show you a direct proof of this; a man can whirl around his head a pail filled with water without its being spilt, and so, in like manner, can the oceans be carried round the Sun without losing a drop. As this illustration was evidently intended to settle the matter, I then said no more upon the subject.[2]

Scott continues his story, but now as a grown, thinking adult who uses critical thinking skills, rather than merely believing what he was taught in school.

> Had such been proposed to me afterwards as a man, I would have answered somewhat as follows—Sir, I beg to say that the illustration you have given of a man whirling a pail of water

---

1. David Wardlaw Scott, *Terra Firma: The Earth Not a Planet, Proved from Scripture, Reason, and Fact* (London, Simpkin, Marshall, Hamilton, Kent, & Col, Ltd., 1901), p. 4.
2. Ibid, p. 1-2.

round his head, and the oceans revolving round the Sun, does not in any degree confirm your argument, because the water in the two cases is placed under entirely different circumstances, but, to be of any value, the conditions in each case must be the same, which here they are not.

The pail is a hollow vessel which holds the water inside it, whereas, according to your teaching, the Earth is a ball, with a continuous curvature outside, which, in agreement with the laws of nature, could not retain any water; besides, as the Scriptures plainly tell us — 2 Pet. 3:5, the water is not contained in the Earth, but the Earth in the water. Again, the man who whirls the pail around his head, takes very good care to hold it straight in an even circuit, for, if he did not, the water would immediately be spilt. But you teach us that the Earth goes upside down and downside up, so that the people in Australia, being on the other side of the so-called Globe, have their feet exactly opposite to ours, for which reason they are named Antipodes. We are not like flies which, by the peculiar conformation of their feet, can crawl on a ball, but we are human beings, who require a plane surface on which to walk; and how could we be fastened to the Earth whirling, according to your theory, around the Sun, at the rate of eighteen miles per second? The famed law of Gravitation will not avail, though we are told that we have fifteen pounds of atmosphere pressing on every square inch of our bodies, but this does not appear to be particularly logical, for there are many athletes who can leap nearly their own height, and run a mile race in less than five minutes, which they could not possibly do were they thus handicapped. Sir, your assertion respecting the revolution of the world round the sun, as illustrated by the pail of water, is utterly worthless, and will never convince any thinking man....[3]

---

3. David Wardlaw Scott, *Terra Firma: The Earth Not a Planet, Proved from Scripture, Reason, and Fact* (London, Simpkin, Marshall, Hamilton, Kent, & Col, Ltd., 1901), p. 2-3.

I don't include these quotes regarding Newton's law of gravitation to either persuade or dissuade you on this subject. The point is to demonstrate how easily one ideology can cancel out other views and become the dominant perceived and accepted truth in society and why it is important for each person to use his or her critical thinking skills to filter and sift through the information presented, regardless of the source.

When it comes to creationism, evolution, intelligent design, or any other theories, people will choose to believe in the ideology that seems most plausible to them.

Regardless of which ideology one decides to embrace—the fact is they cannot all be the absolute truth. Only one can be the truth. If all people believe their ideology is the truth, only one set of people can be correct, while the remaining groups are incorrect. If one group believes humans evolved from fish or monkeys, and another group believes we came from space aliens, and yet another believes that men were created in the image of the supreme one and only God—the fact is that not all beliefs can be correct.

As much as I would like to convince you that my belief in creationism is the absolute truth, unless you embrace my Christian spiritual foundation, it is unlikely you will come to the same conclusion. This is understandable because we come from different life experiences. Notice that my belief on the origin of life is connected to my spiritual foundational beliefs.

Let's go back to the most important question I posed to you earlier, "Think about everything you know … how did you learn what you know?" Remember, I said that it probably is *not* based on *proof* that you yourself saw, touched, smelled, or experienced firsthand.

The origin of life is not the only subject which we've been handed and told to believe. Our form of government is another. Do you know what form of government we have in the United States? What form of government do thought leaders continually speak about? Let's take a look.

## The Democracy Illusion

"The best argument against democracy is a five-minute conversation with the average voter." —Winston Churchill

I'm sitting at my favorite coffee shop as I write this chapter. If I were to approach twenty people randomly and ask them, "What type of government did our Founding Fathers create for the United States?" I am willing to bet that 80 percent would answer, *democratic* or *democracy*.

Why would they answer this way? I believe it is because average citizens hear that our government is a democracy from politicians, professors, and media over and over again. Additionally, young people are brainwashed with this falsehood from primary through graduate school. This has been imprinted on their minds without question. As institutional leaders continually refer to our form of government as a democracy instead of a republic, the human subconscious takes this in and it becomes the truth; but is our government truly a democracy?

In my college American history class our professor taught that a democracy is "mob rule", or rule by the majority; however, the government given to us by our Founding Fathers was a constitutional representative republic. But what do the majority of so-called thought leaders repeat daily? The answer is *democracy*. I suppose to a certain extent it could be called a democracy since for the most part the politicians that supposedly represent us and legislate on our behalf, act like the mob in many instances.

But back to the question, "Why does the majority of Americans believe our form of government is a democracy?"

As demonstrated below, the constant democracy chatter has reverberated across the airwaves and appeared in print for decades upon an unsuspecting American populace who have taken in this non-truth from thought leaders of various political positions. Consider the following:

Nancy Pelosi – in reference to the Trump impeachment issue: "Our democracy is what is at stake... ."[4]

Theodore Roosevelt – "A great democracy has got to be progressive, or it will soon cease to be either great or a democracy."[5]

Ralph Nader – "There cannot be daily democracy without daily citizenship."[6]

Jimmy Carter – "The best way to enhance freedom in other lands is to demonstrate here that our democratic system is worthy of emulation."[7]

George W. Bush – "The roots of our democracy can be traced to England, and to its Parliament... ."[8]

Barack Obama – "There will always be passionate arguments about how we draw the line when it comes to government action. This is how our democracy works."[9]

John McCain – "If you want to preserve—I'm very serious now—if you want to preserve democracy as we know it, you have to have a free and many times adversarial press... ."[10]

What is wrong with a pure democracy?

I referred to a democracy earlier as *mob rule* or the majority of the day—meaning if the majority that rules is no longer a people having good morals, ethics, respect for others, trustworthiness, integrity, etc.—you could end up with a society that is being run by a mob.

4. Reuters.com, *Factbox: Key quotes from U.S. House Speaker Pelosi's statement on impeachment* (Reuters, Dec. 2019).

5. TheodoreRooseveltCenter.org, *The Nation and the States,* speech before the Colorado Legislature, August 29, 1910 (Theodore Roosevelt Center at Dickinson State University).

6. Nader.org, Chapter 3, *The Office of Citizen* (Ralph Nader, Jan. 2004).

7. Jimmy Carter, *Government as Good as Its People* (University of Arkansas Press, Fayetteville 1996), p. 222.

8. NED.org, *Remarks by President George W. Bush at the 20th Anniversary of the National Endowment for Democracy* (United States Chamber of Commerce, Nov. 2003).

9. Barack Obama, *The Audacity of Hope: Thoughts on Reclaiming the American Dream* (Crown Publishers, New York 2006), p. 57.

10. Reuters.com, *Suppressing free press is 'how dictators get started'*: Senator McCain (Reuters, Feb. 2017).

Democracy does not keep everyone free, only the majority. The liberties of the minority in a democracy can be extinguished because it favors only the majority of the day. John Chalfant rationally summed up this point in his book, *Abandonment Theology: The Clergy and the Decline of American Christianity*:

> A pure democracy unbridled and uncontrolled is one of the worst and most unstable forms of government. Karl Marx favored such democracies because they could readily be converted into socialism and then communism. As he (Karl Marx) said in the *Communist Manifesto*, 'The first step in the revolution by the working class ... is to win the battle of democracy.'...
>
> There was not one man among the Founding Fathers who wanted a democracy. Thus, when we are told by our government that the American form of government is a democracy, that statement is not true.[11]

This brings us back to the present day. Case in point: A man at the coffee shop just stopped and asked me what I was writing about so intently. I explained how democracy is not our form of government, and he looked confused. I then explained the difference, and he understood. My point is that most Americans don't know the form of government given to them by the Founding Fathers. Even though most Baby Boomers and GenXers were taught about the constitutional republic form of government—this has been overridden by decades of hearing the word *democracy* when media reports on government and subconsciously, people have absorbed this falsity.

It's not by accident that we hear *democracy* in an echo chamber. In my opinion, it is intentional, but why?

11. John W. Chalfant, *Abandonment Theology: The Clergy and the Decline of American Christianity*, (America: A Call to Greatness, Inc., 1996), p. 15-16.

The reason this has been done is to keep the American people from knowing the real power they were given through the constitutional republic form of government. Not only were they given power, but they were given a responsibility to keep watch over their government in order to keep politicians (supposed public servants) in line and limit government overreach.

Rather than serving the people, our politicians seem to serve their own interests, usually making policy decisions based on which lobbyist group can best line their pockets. The Declaration of Independence that was approved on July 4, 1776, explicitly outlines the power of the people:

> We hold these Truths to be self-evident, that all Men are created equal, that they are endowed by their Creator with certain unalienable Rights, that among these are Life, Liberty, and the pursuit of Happiness—That to secure these Rights, Governments are instituted among Men, deriving their just Powers from the Consent of the Governed, that whenever any Form of Government becomes destructive of these Ends, it is the Right of the People to alter or to abolish it, and to institute new Government, laying its Foundation on such Principles, and organizing its Powers in such Form, as to them shall seem most likely to effect their Safety and Happiness… .[12]

This document stated that the people have the right to alter or abolish a rogue government and institute a new one to effect their safety and happiness. I believe that if any group of people wanted to abolish the current den of thieves in office, they would be labeled domestic terrorists even though it is their right to do so.

If people do not understand the type of government they possess, how can they understand their rights and their duties? The following describes the importance of a republic and why it matters.

12. U.S. Citizenship and Immigration Services, *The Declaration of Independence and the Constitution of the United States,* https://www.uscis.gov/sites/default/files/document/guides/M-654.pdf.

## Understanding the Importance of the Republic

It is important to understand why the constitutional republic was the form of government chosen by the Founding Fathers.

In his book, Chalfant emphasizes how a republic is a unique and stable form of government that gives individuals liberty by its very nature because it was founded upon the righteous laws of God, not men.

"Rather than a democracy, America's government is a republic in which the people elect those who will represent them in performing functions of government … the citizens, in exchange for their God-given freedoms, are charged with the sacred duty of vigilantly watching over their political representatives and of holding them accountable for their public moral conduct and their adherence to Biblical principles in all legislative matters."[13]

A republic—comes with responsibility. As a constitutional republic, it is the responsibility of the people to elect representatives on their behalf, to "represent" their wishes in government—to be the servants of the constituents. On the flip side, the people have the responsibility to ensure the elected representatives are in fact carrying out their wishes. When representatives go off track and start putting their own agenda first, then it is the responsibility of the people to vote them out of office.

Recent generations have been so brainwashed by propaganda, they do not realize they have this power.

Chalfant also discusses another illusion the "wall," referring to the wall of separation between church and state. He reveals how the church's impact in government was removed by this idea of a wall.

"The government was designed to be the servant of the citizens. Any notion of a "wall" limiting the church's direct influence in the legislative or moral affairs of political representatives or institutions preempts the

---

13. John W. Chalfant, *Abandonment Theology: The Clergy and the Decline of American Christianity* (America: A Call to Greatness, Inc., 1996), p. 24.

ability of a citizen to do his sacred duty."[14]

I will expound on the subject of the wall of separation façade and how it began, grew, and fostered the current day churches that ultimately brought us to where we are today—a limping citizenry at best that is *not* carrying out its duty to the republic and a church that has failed the American people and society by becoming part of a government corporation.

Why is it so important to understand and distinguish the difference between democracy and a constitutional republic?

I would argue that first and foremost, if people don't understand their history and the type of government they are a part of, how can they keep it and most of all defend their right to it? I believe this is why the 'talking heads' keep repeating the word *democracy* and why educational institutions quit teaching our real American history. They don't want the younger generations to know about our true form of government, so that the elite establishment can more easily take it away and replace it with a more controlled police state—the mob of our day. I believe many of the problems the *Land of Plenty* is facing, as well as the rest of the world, are based on the fact that the world has lost its spiritual foundation, and this has trickled down through the roots of the different societal institutions.

When a nation founded on biblical principles and accountability to almighty God starts to gut Him from most areas of society, the chaos we are living today is usually the result. When God leaves, the emptiness is replaced by evil and the society rots. The roots of our country's foundation are rotting. I believe that in our country, it is primarily due to the failure of the church.

---

14. John W. Chalfant, *Abandonment Theology: The Clergy and the Decline of American Christianity* (America: A Call to Greatness, Inc., 1996), p. 40.

# CHAPTER 2

# Government and the Church

## Freedom in America Through a Spiritual Foundation

In America today, there's a real divide about what is perceived as a political battle between the Republicans and Democrats. In reality, it is just the minor part of what is an escalated spiritual war—fought on a political and ideological battlefield.

It's not really about Republicans versus Democrats, or one group versus another group. It's really about good versus evil—Satan versus the almighty God, played out on an earthly stage.

America was founded out of the peoples' search for religious freedom and liberty. Founded on biblical principles, the United States was unique in that this was a people who believed their rights and freedom came from God Almighty, not kings or queens.

This argument is stated very clearly in our founding documents. The Declaration of Independence states this explicitly: "… they are endowed by their Creator with certain unalienable Rights… ."[15]

For those who question this line of thinking, I randomly selected a handful of states and took a look at their state constitutions and their preambles, and this is what I found:

---

15. National Archives, America's Founding Documents, The Declaration of Independence, https://www. archives.gov/founding-docs/declaration

## Constitution of the State of Florida: Preamble

"We, the people of the State of Florida, being grateful to almighty God for our constitutional liberty, in order to secure its benefits, perfect our government, insure domestic tranquility, maintain public order, and guarantee equal civil and political rights to all, do ordain and establish this constitution."[16]

## Constitution of the State of California: Preamble

"We, the people of California, grateful to Almighty God for our freedom, in order to secure its blessings, do establish this Constitution."[17]

## Constitution of the State of New York: Preamble

"1 [Preamble] WE THE PEOPLE of the State of New York, grateful to Almighty God for our Freedom, in order to secure its blessings, DO ESTABLISH THIS CONSTITUTION."[18]

## Constitution of the State of Missouri: Preamble

"We, the people of Missouri, with profound reverence for the Supreme Ruler of the Universe, and grateful for His goodness, do establish this Constitution for the better government of the state."[19]

## Constitution of the State of Montana: Preamble

"We the people of Montana, grateful to God for the quiet beauty of our state, the grandeur of our mountains, the vastness of our rolling plains, and desiring to improve the quality of life, equality of opportunity and to secure the blessings of liberty for this and future generations do ordain

---

16. FLSenate.gov, The Florida Senate (*The Florida Constitution*).

17. Leginto.lesgislature.ca.gov, California Legislative Information (*The California Constitution*).

18. Dos.NY.gov, *New York State Constitution*.

19. SOS.MO.gov, Missouri Secretary of State (*The Missouri Constitution*).

and establish this constitution."[20]

These preambles express what was in the hearts of the citizens at the time they were written. In his book, *The Greatest Battle for the Hearts and Minds of Mankind in the History of the World*, author, speaker, and broadcaster Paul McGuire describes the Christian influence on America's foundation that led to the freedom we still experience today:

> America, from the onset of the coming of the Pilgrims and Puritans in the 1600s was imperfect but was a Christian nation built on a belief in the Bible, the Ten Commandments, and the Lord Jesus Christ. In 1776, America became a free nation with a unique Constitution and Bill of Rights ... unlike every other declaration of rights, including European Union and the United Nations, the American Constitution clearly states that our rights are given to us by God and not by man ... they have been granted to us directly by God. No human government has the right to take them away.[21]

It is my opinion that the greatest experiment in the history of the United States was born out of a segment of people with faith in God who came to this country to find freedom to practice their spiritual beliefs, and they built the country's foundation on biblical principles that led to the fulfillment of their dream and prosperity.

Think about the probability in all of history, that such a small group would become the catalyst that led to a nation where everyone in the world wanted to come and try to live their dreams of prosperity and freedom. W. Cleon Skousen, author, teacher, and speaker talks about this small group in his book, *The Making of America: The Substance and Meaning of the Constitution*:

---

20. Leg.MT.gov, *The Constitution of the State of Montana.*

21. Paul McGuire, *The Greatest Battle for the Hearts and Minds of Mankind in the History of the World* (M House Publishers, Los Angeles 2019), p. 77.

This book is about the world's greatest political success formula. In a little over a century, this formula allowed a small segment of the human family—less than six percent—to become the richest industrial nation on earth. It allowed them to originate more than half of the world's total production and enjoy the highest standard of living in the history of the world.

It also produced a very generous people. No nation in all the recorded annals of the past has shared so much of its wealth with every other nation as has the United States of America.[22]

Could it be that the God of the Bible, the God of Abraham, Isaac, and Jacob, put this burning desire in the hearts of the people in this small group so that they would break away from England, come to a new land, and start shaping a free nation that would spiritually minister to its own people, and then minister to other nations around the world? This could have never happened under a closed, un-free society.

Freedom is only possible when a government that allows spiritual goodness produces a civil, moral people and society. Tyranny is the byproduct of a spiritually bankrupt society where government keeps out spiritual goodness and righteousness, and it produces an enslaved, controlled, poor, and miserable people.

A free society rarely stays free for long when it forgets its moral compass; we are currently witnessing the downfall of the United States. As the trajectory of removing a spiritual foundation goes up in our society, so does the chaos.

In the spiritual realm, I believe that Satan is currently hard at work stamping out the spiritual goodness in our society as he moves us into a society of depravity. I believe that for every good action taken by almighty God, Satan mimics those actions in a purely evil way. As an antithesis of

22. W. Cleon Skousen, *The Making of America: The Substance and Meaning of the Constitution* (Washington: The National Center for Constitutional Studies, 1985), p. 1.

every good action, he takes an evil action. This has been and is now clearly manifesting in our physical world.

I spoke about the founding of the United States and the peoples' acknowledgment of their Creator in the founding documents. At the same time, I believe Satan was forming his own counter strategy through a vehicle that is known as the *Illumined Ones*.

## The Founding Antithesis, Illumined Ones

Now if you believe that we've always been and are in a spiritual battle since the fall of Adam and Eve in the garden of Eden—you understand that the devil is real and he always creates a counterfeit to everything good that almighty God creates. This being said, not so coincidentally, also in 1776, as America became a free nation, there was the creation of another powerful organization—brought into existence to specifically destroy anything of God, Christianity, and a free people of any kind. This group is what I refer to as the "founding antithesis" called the Illuminati (meaning the enlightened ones).

You may have heard people use the terms, *the elite, the establishment,* or *those in charge* when discussing the people in charge of all things political at the local, regional, and global levels. The establishment, as I understand it, is the world power broker group originally founded by the big banking families.

McGuire's *Greatest Battle* describes how the group we've come to know as the Illuminati (or the elites in charge) came to power:

> In 1776, the world's most powerful secret occult organization,
> the Illuminati, was also founded with the enormous power
> of international banking families like the Rothschild family.
> The Illuminati despised the concept of a free nation and a free

people who believe that their rights have been given to them by God!

The Illuminati and other secret societies are all built on the satanic idea that it is the birthright of what is called "Illuminati bloodline families" to rule and reign over the masses as 'god-kings' and that they have the right to make the rest of mankind their slaves … almost every empire and kingdom, even all kingdoms of European governments and empires, have been created for the purpose of enslaving the masses for the benefit of the secret occult elite.[23]

Now, revisiting the idea of a spiritual battle—we are not really fighting the Illuminati, big bankers, despots, communists, political leaders, political parties, world leaders, etc. These are the physical vehicles used on earth to wage the spiritual war against anything or anyone God-fearing, righteous, or good—and against our freedom and liberties, in order to enslave and control people everywhere. This is the goal of the devil—to keep people separated from their Creator forever.

Since this is a spiritual war against good, it makes sense that we are seeing more persecution of Christians daily on a worldwide scale. Much of the mainstream media makes fun of Christians and calls them intolerant bigots to demonize them in the eyes of the half-asleep public.

Why do they continually tear down Christianity? They would never do this to Islam—as it would be very politically incorrect. But why isn't it politically incorrect to insult Christians? It's not only okay; it is almost touted as the thing to do to be cool.

To answer these questions, it is again because this is a spiritual battle against the almighty God.

If you step back and look at the founding of the United States and

23. Paul McGuire, *The Greatest Battle for the Hearts and Minds of Mankind in the History of the World* (M House Publishers, Los Angeles 2019), p. 77-78.

realize it was brought into existence to establish freedom of religion (by Christians) but simultaneously gave us a way of life based on freedom and liberties, it makes sense that this way of life has to be destroyed if the endgame is to enslave people. The U.S. has been the beacon of light in terms of freedom for the world. If the U.S. goes down, everyone goes down with it.

If you question this, ask yourself why people are trying to illegally enter the U.S. in droves. Why aren't people clamoring to get into countries like Mexico, Iran, Iraq, or even the socialist Sweden that we hear so much about?

No matter their gender, religion, ethnicity—people intrinsically want to be free. This is not by accident. Our Creator made His people this way—it is who and what they are.

## From Illumination to Socialism

The recent fascination with socialism in America is also not by accident. It is just another vehicle in the arsenal the self-described "elites" used to bring down freedom.

McGuire explains how political ideologies are purposely used to destroy Christianity and ultimately freedom: "The fact that socialism, communism, Marxism, and occult forces are organized and aggressively at work to take over society and to completely destroy Christianity should be obvious to anyone with a minimal knowledge of history."[24]

He goes on to quote Karl Marx, author of the *Communist Manifesto*. If you have a doubt about how powerful a role Christianity has played in keeping people free, read the following quote by Marx—even he realized the power: "Our war is against the Christian God and the world created by Him."[25]

---

24. Paul McGuire, *The Greatest Battle for the Hearts and Minds of Mankind in the History of the World* (M House Publishers, Los Angeles 2019), p. 29.

25. Ibid, p. 29.

And to help us understand Marx's spiritual stance and how it was in line with his worldview, McGuire includes: "Thus heaven I've forfeited; I know it full well; my soul once true to God; is chosen for hell!"[26]

I am astounded by the recent acceptance of socialism in the United States. In school, we were taught that socialism and communism were used to deny people the things that gave them the power to live free: from owning personal property; choosing how they wanted to make their living; what jobs they wanted; to practicing the religion they wanted; owning a business, and freely moving about from state to state.

Now it seems the younger generations, more specifically starting with the Millennial generation, have been taught the opposite of these once-believed tenets. Younger people seem to embrace socialism and believe it will solve society's problems. The irony is that this same generation has had life easy compared historically to former generations since the founding of the United States.

They walk around with iPhones (that now cost upwards of $1,000) made by a capitalist economy, sipping on $4 lattes, while complaining about how horrible our capitalist society is. Yet they fully participate in it and enjoy it.

It's been awhile since I learned about Karl Marx in school, so I decided to do research to refresh my memory. What I found is very much in step with some of today's political thinking.

## The Ironies of Marxism, Socialism, and Communism

Interestingly, Karl Marx, known as the father of communism, was born in Germany and was the son of a successful, wealthy lawyer. Note: Ironically Marx's father must have been a hardworking man to have been a success in his field.

---

26. Ibid, p. 29.

Marx attended school away from home—also indicative that his family must have had monetary assets to send him away for higher education at that time.

In 1958, former Director of the Federal Bureau of Investigation, J. Edgar Hoover, wrote an interesting account about the insidious leaders behind the takedown of freedom in his book, *Masters of Deceit*.

The following gives you some indication as to the type of person Marx was:

"… After graduation, he did not have a job and did not seem to care to find one—another lifelong trait. He dabbled in atheism, social-ism, and polemics … Marx had become an atheist and called for war against religion, a war that was to become the cornerstone of communist philosophy."[27]

Hoover goes on to describe the poverty and pitiful state that Marx lived in by his own doing—even though he had a wife and several children. Hoover talks about how Marx would not work a real job, but was quick to complain and blame capitalism for the poverty and squalor in which he found himself.

He makes this point about Marx in the following passage: "… Marx was stubborn. He kept plugging away, writing, reading, denouncing capi-talist poverty, and letting his family starve."[28]

As previously stated, Marx came from a family of means that was able to send him to college. Many millennials have also come from situations that have afforded them the opportunity to attend higher education. In both of these scenarios, it is a capitalist system that has allowed them to get a college education. However, both Marx and a majority of millennials also reject the capitalist system that gave them opportunity and instead

---

27. J. Edgar Hoover, *Masters of Deceit: The Story of Communism in America and How to Fight It* (Henry Hold and Company, Inc., 1958), p. 14.

28. Ibid., p. 17.

embrace socialism, a system that stifles opportunity and economic growth.

Hoover's book shows that Marx seemed to depend on others for his material means throughout his life. A wealthy uncle semi-supported him, and Marx accepted help from his long-time colleague, Friedrich Engels. He met and befriended this like-minded gentleman, and they collaborated for many years.

"Marx did not have a regular job but depended on pittances from Engels. He lived from pawnshop to pawnshop. It is a bitter irony of history, indeed, that the founder of communism should be literally kept alive by a wealthy industrialist, and that a 'capitalist's' son, turned communist, should become the second father of this revolutionary movement."[29]

As I read Hoover's account of Marx, and as I mentioned earlier, many of this recent generation have often grown up in 'well-to-do' situations. Isn't it again ironic how they also embrace a philosophy that depends on others and do not want to take responsibility for their own social and economic place in society. They believe it would be utopian to rely on a system of government that steps in and takes care of everything for them—thus releasing or absolving them of having to do the work for themselves.

Of course, when I write this about the millennial generation, it does not include *all* millennials—there are, thank God, exceptions. This is a general observation that speaks to some similarities in upbringing and explains why they seem to gravitate to this ideology.

Another irony regarding Engels, Marx's colleague: While coming from a family that was wealthy due to capitalism, Engels rejected his father's example and became an atheist and a communist. Hoover describes him here:

"Engels, a vivid contrast to the morose and crotchety Marx, was gay,

---

29. Ibid., p. 15.

mannerly, from a wealthy family, and interested in having a good time. He too was an atheist and a revolutionary, a fact that deeply offended his father, a leading textile manufacturer and churchman. He would provide money for school, the elder Engels said, but none for revolutionary activities."[30]

Hoover sums up another irony regarding the work and life of Marx and his march against the supposed capitalist tyrant system that he pontificated about unceasingly. "This man who attacked the domination of the capitalists showed his own dominating nature again and again. In theory, he was 'for' the common man and wanted to correct the ills of society. In practice, his fanatical intolerance and overbearing ego made him a tyrant, an autocrat, a dictator."[31]

When I came across this example of the pot calling the kettle black, it reminded me of another modern-day socialism promoter who has bashed people of wealth and ran for president as a candidate of the Democrat party—Bernie Sanders.

## Socialism: Same Old Story, New Players

Bernie Sanders is a guy who frequently tears down wealthy people but he has made a pocketful of money rather recently and quickly as stated in this CNN news article titled: "How Bernie Sanders Became a Millionaire":

"… (tax) returns provided by his campaign in April 2019, Sanders and wife Jane's bottom line jumped from $240,622 in 2015, the year he launched his first White House bid to $1,083,333 a year later, as the once obscure lawmaker became a political sensation on the left and a bestselling author with royalties pouring in … Sanders and his wife made total of more than $2.79 million, putting him in the category of the super-rich."[32]

30. Ibid., p. 15.

31. Ibid., p. 22-23.

32. CNN.com, "How Bernie Sanders Became a Millionaire" (CNN, orig. publication Apr. 2019).

Isn't this rich? (pun intended)

There is nothing wrong with Sanders writing a bestseller, but how will he justify this to his socialist groupies? How will he explain that he's made a stack of cash rather quickly in a capitalist environment. Do you see yet another socialist irony?

Here is a man who has designed his political platform around chastising the rich and insinuating how this makes them greed monsters, while he himself has been catapulted into the 'Millionaires Club'—and seems to be quite comfortable in this capitalist camp. What does he tell his supporters now? "Do what I say, *not* as I do?"

As I was writing about these many ironies, I could not help but see the parallels. Capitalism breeds hard work and production; rejects government dependence; and instead relies on the belief in a higher power—in most cases, specifically on almighty God.

Meanwhile socialism and communism breed as little work as possible and look to embrace and rely on government dependence because the socialist/communist system is their god. They reject a higher power.

This is an example of the point I expressed in the preface of this book: Our political beliefs seem to be, for the most part, related to our spiritual beliefs—and in turn, define who we truly are.

## Globalism: Same Old Story, Same Players

In America, the globalists have kept a hold on the people, while many are still under the impression that they are free; they are slowly losing more freedoms every day. Some are starting to wake up to this fact.

It is my opinion that the globalist elite keep a hold indefinitely on the people by letting them think they vote for those in charge from the federal government (President, Senate, Congress) and state governments down to the local government actors.

Just after 9/11, journalist Francie Grace of *CBS News* reported about a group of governmental insiders who stand by to run the show should there be an emergency. How many Americans are aware of this?

Grace revealed the following in her report titled, "'Shadow Government' News to Congress" in March 2002:

> A 'shadow government' consisting of 75 or more senior officials has been living and working secretly outside Washington since September 11th in case the nation's capital is crippled by a terrorist attack.
>
> Under the classified "Continuity of Operations Plan," which was first reported by *The Washington Post* in its Friday editions, high-ranking officials representing their departments have begun rotating in and out of the assignment at one of two fortified locations along the east coast.
>
> The underground government would try to contain disruptions of the nation's food and water supplies, transportation links, energy and telecommunications networks, public health and civil order, the Post reported. Later, it would begin to reconstitute the government.[33]

Harry Helms, author of *Inside the Shadow Government: National Emergencies and the Cult of Secrecy*, expands on what he calls, "the true scope and awesome potential" of this shadow government: "It also includes plans for detention and arrest—without probable cause or warrant—of American citizens, government control of all radio and television stations, seizure of private property (including cars) and bank accounts, and the use of U.S. military to impose martial law and conduct combat operations in American cities if the President declares a national emergency."[34]

33. CBSNews.com, 'Shadow Government' News to Congress, Francie Grace, March 1, 2002. https://www.cbsnews.com/news/shadow-government-news-to-congress/.

34. Harry Helms, *Inside the Shadow Government: National Emergencies and the Cult of Secrecy* (Feral House, Los Angeles, 2003), p. 2.

Helms goes on to say that under this shadow government, the president can suspend the Constitution and Bill of Rights—through an executive order.

Although Helms says the shadow government and associated powers were inflated due to the September 11 terrorist attacks, this is not where the shadow government originated. He claims that, "Much of the 'Shadow Government' infrastructure, such as the underground shelters used after September 11, was constructed during the Eisenhower and Kennedy years."[35]

As it seems with many of the actions put into place in the name of fighting terrorism, they seem to be directed more toward clamping down on U.S. citizens and their rights, rather than containing or ending terrorism.

On the morning of September 11, like everyone else, I was in shock at first and did not know what to make of everything. When the dust settled, I realized that President Bush was *not* shutting down the southern U.S. border to keep potential terrorists out of the country—this is when I thought that more was going on than we were led to believe.

I now had to go through searches at the airport and could not carry shampoo or nail clippers, but terrorists could walk across the southern border.

Helms makes the claim that the shadow government is not controlled by a secret cabal. This may have been true in its earlier days, but I would not be so quick to agree that this is the case now.

He states in the report that most of America probably agrees that there is a need for an in-place contingency plan in case of an attempted national takeover or other emergency. I don't dispute this reasoning, but I question who is in charge of putting this contingency plan in place and why. I think this is especially important now, in light of all of the bad actors who

---

35. Ibid., p. 2.

have reared their heads the last few decades in government, the judiciary, media, entertainment, big business, education, healthcare, etc.

I agree with Helms that the U.S. "has no need for a Shadow Government… we already have a 'Sunshine Government' defined by the Constitution and implemented by laws passed by elected representation of the American people."[36]

He said that any contingency plan for an emergency situation can already be accommodated within the current Constitution and government framework.

I would add that since the current government is corrupt enough, why would we willingly welcome a secret auxiliary government to install itself in its place during an emergency? The people would be taking a great risk by trusting such a move. The history of mankind has proven that some leaders cannot be trusted in the long run, especially when it comes to power and control.

Even though I am a Christian, I have been vocal about my opinion that society is largely in a sad state because Christian church pastors have been silent for the most part on many moral issues for decades. This is because many sold out to the government and helped them build the wall of separation—an invented concept found nowhere in our founding documents—between the church and society and its people.

The Founding Fathers were quite aware of the responsibility the church had to keep a free, civil, and moral society.

"It is the duty of the clergy to accommodate their discourses to the times, to preach against such sins as are most prevalent, and recommend such virtues as are most wanted." —John Adams

---

36. Ibid., p. 20.

# Wall of Separation and the 501c3 Church

Those in charge understand the role of the church and how important it is in terms of preserving freedom, morality, and a prosperous society. So if the end game is to destroy the United States, there had to be a strategy to tear down this nation. This is where the invention of the 501c3 church comes into play.

# What Is the 501c3 Church and Why Does It Matter?

The 501c3 church is simply a status the government issues to a church that signs on to its corporation system in exchange for a tax exempt status, thereby releasing the church from any responsibility to pay taxes on the monies that come into the church from its members.

No discussion about the tax-exempt 501c3 church would be complete without first giving a background and history on the false idea of a wall of separation that has been cleverly ingrained into the minds of an unsuspecting American people.

Let's start with the "wall of separation" Chalfant spoke about in his book.

What is it? It is the idea that there is and always was a "wall of separation" between the government and the church in America so that a government church could not be established as was the Church of England that had power to tell people how to worship. This catalyst pushed a God-fearing people to come to America so they could worship freely whom and how they wanted to worship without government interference.

The only problem is a "wall of separation" was never mentioned in the Declaration of Independence, the Bill of Rights, or the Constitution.

As I showed earlier, in the state Preambles, God-fearing people established their governments based on their Christian principles that they brought with them. Again, it is my opinion that our spiritual foundational principles are intrinsic to our political beliefs and tenets—they make up who and what we are. This explains that when these people came to America, they naturally weaved their spiritual principles into their political and governmental foundations.

This is not different from Islamic countries; their religious tenets are not separate from their governmental laws and tenets. They are melded together in their societies.

I would also contend that communist countries are no different except that their religion is atheism—no belief in a god. Their governments are based on secularism and are void of almighty God. No god is included in their spiritual lives or governments.

I am not saying Christians came to America to establish a Christian-only society. In fact, it is quite the opposite. Christianity is different in that it is based on free will and the gift of freedom. While they weaved Christian principles into their governments, it was for the purpose of allowing all people in America to use their free will to practice the religion of their choice, or to practice no religion, and to be free as to whom, what, and how they worshiped.

This is precisely why in the Bill of Rights, the First Amendment clearly states—"Congress shall make no law respecting an establishment of religion"—in other words, no state-endorsed church could be established. And the amendment continues, " … or prohibiting the free exercise thereof."[37] This clearly states the people are free to participate in the religion of their choice. They even have the freedom *not* to participate in a religion.

In other words, the entire system of government, the American government, was originally designed around the idea of freedom. Founders took

---

37. Archives.gov, National Archives, America's Founding Documents, The Bill of Rights: A Transcription.

the gift God gave them and brought it into their society. Again, you can see from this example that their religion and politics are not separated.

So if they are not separated, where did this wall of separation mantra come from? Chalfant explains in his book how this idea came from a letter Thomas Jefferson wrote to the Danbury Baptist Association:

> The responsibility of 'We the People,' the citizens of America, to ensure that the righteous are in authority has been dangerously hampered by the introduction of a single concept: the "wall of separation" between church and state.
>
> In 1947, Justice of the U.S. Supreme Court Hugo Black (in Everson v. Board of Education) declared that such a wall must exist between the church and the state. He had taken out of context and expression from Thomas Jefferson's letter to the Danbury Baptist Association previously mentioned, written years after the First Amendment had been ratified. The Court apparently ignored the true notion of Jefferson's "wall" illustration—that a wall must exist to forbid the government from intruding into the affairs of the church. Justice Black, with no precedent, decided that the reverse was also necessary—that the church must not be involved with the affairs of state. Jefferson's "wall" was a one-way wall; the court's was a two-way wall. In fact, there is no mention of the words *church* or *separation* in the First Amendment or in the body of the Constitution, and the word *state* is used only in reference to states' rights, not the separation issue...
>
> The government was designed to be the servant of the citizens. Any notion of a "wall" limiting the church's direct influence in the legislative or moral affairs of political representatives or institutions preempts the ability of a citizen to do his sacred duty.[38]

---

38. John W. Chalfant, *Abandonment Theology: The Clergy and the Decline of American Christianity* (America: A Call to Greatness, Inc., 1996), p. 39-40.

I believe this move by the court was merely a way to hoodwink the people into believing the church could not be involved in political issues. This was an insidious way to muzzle the church leaders from calling out wrongdoing of government, government officials, and politicians. It was always supposed to be the role of the people to keep watch and address wrongdoing in government—whether people are part of a church of not. This is a tenet of the republic if the people are to remain free; otherwise, as noted earlier in this book, you end up with 'mob rule.'

So, if you repeat a lie often, it becomes ingrained in the minds of people, and they accept it as truth. This has been the case since the 1947 court decision.

Now that we've reviewed the improperly and falsely established wall of separation, let's get back to the 501c3 church.

The 501c3 is a tax-exempt status given to religious and other nonprofit organizations. The irony is that the church was never under an obligation to pay taxes in the first place. The First Amendment established that religious beliefs were a "free" expression and were in no way under a government stranglehold and therefore could not be taxed—the church was automatically tax exempt. (Remember: First Amendment: " Congress shall make no law respecting an establishment of religion, or prohibiting the free exercise thereof... ."[39]

If the church was automatically tax-exempt, why are the majority of churches under the 501c3 status today?

The 501c3 status was like the 1947 wall of separation court decision. It was another vehicle used to shut down the church from speaking out negatively about the government leaders or politicians.

The first thing to understand is that *no* church is required to sign up for 501c3 status; churches that sign up are doing it voluntarily.

---

39. Archives.gov, National Archives, America's Founding Documents, The Bill of Rights: A Transcription.

It is important to know that if a church does *not* sign up for 501c3 status, it automatically has the freedom to call out government and political officials for wrongdoing. If government leaders are involved in immoral or illegal activity, church leaders can boldly speak out against them. Historically, this was a way to keep politicians in line; otherwise, they knew the spotlight would put attention on their wrongdoings. This could result in losing votes of church members.

Seven years after the wall of separation scheme, another was created to muzzle church leaders. In 1954, Senator Lyndon B. Johnson decided he wanted to shut the mouths of church leaders and curtail their influence on potential constituents and political agendas. He came up with the 501c3 church tax-exempt status scheme.

Author and speaker Richard D. Proctor, PhD, reviews the insidious plan of LBJ in his book, *Liberty, Will It Survive the 21st Century?* Volume 2 … article from *Heal Our Ministries*:

> Most churches in America have organized as '501c3 tax-exempt religious organizations.' This is a fairly recent trend that has only been going on for about fifty years. Churches were only added to section 501c3 of the tax code in 1954. We can thank Sen. Lyndon B. Johnson for that. Johnson was no ally of the church. As part of his political agenda, Johnson had it in mind to silence the church and eliminate the significant influence the church had always had on shaping public policy.
>
> Although Johnson proffered this as a "favor" to churches, the favor also came with strings attached … 501c3 churches are prohibited from addressing, in any tangible way, the vital issues of the day.
>
> The 501c3 has had a "chilling effect" upon the free speech rights of the church. LBJ was a shrewd and cunning politician who

seemed to well-appreciate how easily many of the clergy would sell out.

Did the church ever need to seek permission from the government to be exempt from taxes? Were churches prior to 1954 taxable? No, churches have never been taxable.[40]

Once organizations sign up for this status, they forfeit their free speech rights against any negative political or governmental agenda. How could he convince church leaders to sign up voluntarily for this status? LBJ sold it to them as a benefit; they would be tax-exempt (which, ironically, they already were) and their congregations could deduct church donations from their taxes. It worked like a charm and gained steam to this day as most churches believe that when they form, they are *required* to sign up for a 501c3 status. Remember what I said about repeating a lie over and over. Signing up for 501c3 status is *not* required; it is a purely voluntary action.

So now for nearly seventy years, we've had churches that cannot speak out on government or political wrongdoing for a benefit they already had. This has resulted in a society that is morally bankrupt with gangster politicians living under 'mob rule.' This is precisely what LBJ wanted—a muzzled church.

Even the Internal Revenue Service code states that the church is automatically exempt from taxation. IRS Code 508 (C) (1) (A)

"(C) Exceptions

(1)Mandatory exceptions Subsections (a) and (b) shall not apply to—

(A) Churches, their integrated auxiliaries, and conventions or associations of churches … "[41]

---

40. Richard D. Proctor PhD, *Liberty Will It Survive? the 21st Century? Volume 2* (Provis Press, 2016), p. 105.

41. Law.Cornell.edu, Cornell Law School, Legal Information Institute, 26 U.S. Code § 508. Special rules with respect to section 501c3 organizations.

According to Peter Kershaw's *In Caesar's Grip*, even those who work for the IRS have wondered why churches are signing up for their own demise:

> I am not the only IRS employee who's wondered why churches go to the government and seek permission to be exempted from a tax they didn't owe to begin with, and to seek a tax deductible status that they've always had anyway. Many of us have marveled at how church leaders want to be regulated and controlled by an agency of government that most Americans have prayed would just get out of their lives. Churches are in an amazingly unique position, but they don't seem to know or appreciate the implications of what it would mean to be free of government control... .[42] —Steve Nestor, Retired IRS Sr. Revenue Officer

I've made two major points on the 501c3 church tax exempt status issue:

1) It is voluntary; not required.
2) When a church signs up for 501c3 status, it loses its right to speak out against political agents or agendas.

Before I close on this subject, there is one more important point to be made. I interviewed Christopher Johnson of Creation Liberty Evangelism back in 2013 on the 501c3 church. Aside from the tax exemption and free speech issues, he made what might actually be the most important point.

Before a church signs up for 501c3 status, it is a free church under the almighty God with Jesus Christ being the head of the church. Johnson said that when a church signs up for the 501c3 tax-exempt status, it is in reality signing a contract to join the government as a "state" church; it can *no longer* be under Christ, but is now under the government—the state now becomes its master.

Johnson made the following statement as he paraphrased an article

---

42. Peter Kershaw, *In Caesar's Grip* (Heal Our Land Ministries, 2000) p. II. http://jcmatthews.org/uploads/5/3/7/7/5377341/in_caesars_grip.pdf

from the Biblical Law Center regarding what happens when a church has a signed contract with the state and becomes a state-ruled corporation:

"I want you to listen very carefully when you get 501c3 incorporated - that means you are incorporated and even as a member of a church, you are part of that corporation ... your church signed a contract, he (your pastor) signed it over because according to that contract your pastor is considered the CEO of that corporation, he signed a contract stating the creator of the church is the state not God, the state is the sole authority...."[43]

In our interview, Johnson followed up this statement with a scripture from Matthew 6:24 that states a church or its people cannot serve two masters: "Jesus Christ said no man can serve two masters, for either he will hate the one and love the other or else you will hold onto the one and despise the other ... you cannot serve God and mammon. Folks, mammon was the money of their day ... you can't serve God but at the same time have signed a contract for money."[44]

So have churches that have signed up for 501c3 status signed up for the money, either knowingly or unknowingly? Does this excuse them from their responsibility to God?

Here is what I know: Christ is over the church. And in my opinion, the original role of the church in terms of money was *not* to raise millions of dollars to purchase or build huge worship centers with gymnasiums or to buy private jets. Is this really why pastors sign onto 501c3 status, to create a nontaxable safety net for their high-priced purchases in case they are audited at some point?

I believe that collected monies were originally intended to help those members in the church such as the elderly, widows with children, or the

---

43. The Truth Seekers Radio Show: Episode 4; Christopher Johnson author and speaker of "Christian Liberty Evangelism," 2013.

44. Ibid.

sick and infirm who could not work.

As I was finishing this chapter on the "wall of separation" and 501c3, it struck me as funny that the same 1947 court decision that created this "wall" was an off-shoot of the same government that is signing up churches under 501c3 status to join the government as a state-ruled corporation—so much for their wall of separation argument.

## Discussing Politics and Religion

As I spoke about earlier in the preface to this book, why is it that in a "free" society we have been told over and over again that there are two things you should not discuss—politics and religion?

As our constitutional republic gets older, we see fewer people discussing these topics in both public and private settings. We won't discuss it with family or friends when we get together for the holidays because it might cause hurt feelings, or worse, a fight that may separate us from loved ones indefinitely—how sad.

According to Dr. Richard D. Proctor, PhD, avoiding discussions of politics and religion among individuals may have started around the same time the church quit discussing political issues in the pulpit. In 1954, when Senator Lyndon B. Johnson devised his plan to trick the clergy into silence, Dr. Proctor states the people may have followed the church's lead: "Sometime during this same period, churches began the custom of not discussing politics in their classes or environments. And the people at large began the custom of not discussing either politics or religion."[45]

Self-censorship really seemed to escalate and take hold during the Clinton administration when the 'politically correct' mantra was put into motion in the 1990's.

If we are a free people in a free society, why can't we discuss the sub-

---

45. Richard D. Proctor PhD, *Liberty Will It Survive? The 21st Century Volume 2* (Provis Press, 2016), p. 106.

jects of politics and religion in a civil manner? Why is this lie hammered over and over again? We hear this edict from the media gods—and most recently in electronic form—so that it has subconsciously become a hands-off topic.

Media and government giants have built up this layer of *fear* to keep us from these discussions because they fear that we may find we agree on some points, or worse, we might open someone else's eyes to truth. This is the reason this censorship monster was created.

Self-censorship is dangerous because it is a strategy to divide people in the United States, to put each group of people in a particular box, and then to pit them one against the other. This has to be done to divide the American people so that those in control can successfully ruin this country and overtake it with their globalist agenda. Until they divide the people, they cannot take it over.

Regardless of your personally-held views or values, whether you are politically left, right, or center, whether you embrace a religious worldview or a secularist ideology—these views come from your internal barometer—the foundation that is deeply embedded into what makes up your being—your character. These beliefs can develop or even change over time; however, the point is that the beliefs are an extension, an outward expression of you and who you are—what makes up you, your personality, how you conduct your life, your behavior, your speech, your interactions with others. The beliefs make up your essence. When I hear that these subjects are taboo, I believe they are saying they want to extinguish *you*.

When I meet people and I want to get to know about them, my curiosity about their beliefs tells me immediately, although not exclusively, a lot about those people even without an in-depth discussion. Even if we don't agree on political and religious views, I want to know more about them and what experiences brought them to those beliefs. This is nothing more than wanting to truly get to know people even if we don't agree. It is not about how I can start a fight or argument with them, but how we can have an interesting discussion. Maybe ultimately the discussions can bring us to consensus on an issue. But this is what the fearmongers want to discourage.

No matter what your beliefs or views, I encourage you to share and discuss them rather than censor them. When we self-censor, we become less free with each passing day.

# CHAPTER 3

# The Central Banking System and Money

*"Let me control a people's currency and I care not who makes their laws."*
— Meyer Nathaniel Rothschild, 1912

## The Federal Reserve Banking Cartel

When the average person thinks of money, he or she really thinks about whether there is enough to cover monthly expenses for specific needs, or wants, or for savings. Rarely does a person worry about the history of the banking system, how it ties into our society, and why it will be important in terms of the future of America and people around the world.

My public school education was void of anything about banking. As I started to discover who runs the banking system, I found they also ran the corporations; they controlled politicians, and the world. It made sense that the banking system and Federal Reserve would not be a focus of public education's curricula. If they taught people the truth about money and banking, they might never have gotten as far as they have with their control agenda.

Let's take a look at some historical banking information. In another volume of Dr. Richard Proctor's writings, he lays out how the banking elite started early in U.S. history to stomp on the Constitution, which allowed them to build a money system they control until this day:

The Constitution was ratified June 21, 1778. The ink was barely dry when one of the major infringements of it occurred. That infringement was the chartering of the First Bank of the United States which was organized in 1791 and chartered for 20 years. It was a central bank that was patterned after the central banks that existed at the time in Europe. Those banks were all controlled by the Rothschild family and their associates, as was ours. That bank was given complete authority over all financial activities of our nation.[46]

Proctor goes on to describe how this was a deliberate violation of the U.S. Constitution that had originally instilled power to create and value currency in the U.S. House of Representatives. This Congressional power to coin money was now siphoned off by a centralized banking system.

Coining money is another responsibility of Congress. Coining of money means the creation of that actual item called money whether it is coin or paper. That includes establishing the monetary levels of dollars in our country and then producing it in whatever denominations desired.

They have abrogated that obligation, power, or authority and gave it to a privately owned central bank called the Federal Reserve which is owned and controlled by foreign banking interests which were and are mostly European.[47]

A group of elite and rich men knew if they wanted to control the government and the people, they'd have to create and control the money system. In 1789, Alexander Hamilton was put in charge of the U.S. Treasury. He advocated creating a national bank and presented a plan to Congress in 1790 to urge its establishment.

Despite opposition, Congress ultimately passed the bill, and President

46. Richard D. Proctor PhD, *Liberty, Will It Survive the 21st Century?* Volume 5 (Provis Press, 2016), p. 9.

47. Richard D. Proctor PhD, *Liberty, Will It Survive the 21st Century? Volume 5* (Provis Press, 2016), p. 11.

Washington signed it into law on February 25, 1791. The First Bank of the United States operated until its charter expired in 1811, and it was followed by the Second Bank of the United States until 1836.[48] The powerbrokers continued to create charters for U.S. banks and renewed them until finally in 1836, they were denied renewal. In 1913, out of frustration, the hoodwink continued as this group of rich and powerful bankers got together and created the Federal Reserve. This banking cartel oversees all the banks that are part of a national United States central banking system. The initial attempt to create this system in the early 1900s was unsuccessful. W. Cleon Skousen, author of *The Naked Capitalist,* states the reason for this:

"It was introduced into the Senate as the Aldrich Bill. The name Aldrich was so closely linked to Morgan and Wall Street, and the resentment against these influences was so strong, that the bill was readily defeated. The group of master planners backed away to devise a new tactic."[49]

Apparently, the designers of the plan felt the public perception was that the Republican party was too closely associated with Wall Street, so to get the new plan adopted, their strategy was to get the Democrats into power and get a new bill passed through them.

Some things never change. As you can see, the rich and powerful have been playing this same game for decades, making the people think there is a difference between Republicans and Democrats, while all along, the rich and powerful control both sides.

The election of 1912 was no different. The banking cartel had to take control of both parties for their strategy to work. The incumbent was President Taft (Republican); he was known to oppose the banksters'

---

48. Philadelphia Encyclopedia; First Bank of the United States, by Jordan AP Fansler https://philadelphiaencyclopedia.org/essays/bank-of-the-united-states-first/.

49. *The Naked Capitalist* by W. Cleon Skousen, including excerpts from *Tragedy and Hope* by Carroll Quigley. Verity Publishing, 1970, p. 18.

bill. The cartel had to bring someone in to cut him out of the picture; Republican Theodore Roosevelt was the guy. They also brought in and backed Woodrow Wilson for the Democrat seat.

Taking control of the 1912 presidential election by controlling two of the three candidates was one of the tricks they played. They even pumped money into creating a phony citizens group (National Citizens League for the Promotion of a Sound Banking System) that would be portrayed as a supporter of the centralized bank system. As they usually do, the elite establishment created, manipulated, and succeeded by controlling many moving parts to get The Federal Reserve Act passed in 1913.

The Federal Reserve System, also known as The Fed, has always had a mystique about it. If you ask the average person on the street what he or she knows about the Fed, most often you will hear that it is an arm of the government that is responsible for the U.S. Treasury.

According to Proctor, not only is the Federal Reserve *not* part of the federal government, it is a privately-owned bank and the U.S. government has *no* say in the Federal Reserve's actions:

"The Federal Reserve is a private corporation owned by the major United States banks which are in turn owned by the major banks of Europe which are in turn owned by the International Banking Establishment... . The Federal Reserve has a monopoly on the banking system ... this organization is a foreign private corporation which now oversees and controls our lives. It decides how much money will be created and our representative government does not have any say whatsoever in its operations."[50]

So the Federal Reserve is part of a larger privately-owned corporation and system of central banks both domestic and international. They create money, set its value, and can put it into the system at will with absolutely

---

50. Richard D. Proctor, PhD, *Liberty, Will It Survive? The 21st Century Volume 1* (Provis Press, 2016), p. 70-71.

no U.S. government oversight. Not only is there no government oversight, this Central Bank System holds governments hostage around the world and rules over their actions on a worldwide scale.

Skousen also casts light on the Federal Reserve international banking connection: "… to use the financial power of Britain and the United States to force all the major countries to operate through central banks free from all political control, with all questions of international finance to be settled by agreements by such central banks without interference from governments."[51]

Skousen summarizes the views of professor Dr. Carroll Quigley, author of *Tragedy and Hope*, and claims Quigley intentionally wanted to unveil details about the Central Banking cartel to let people know who is running the world:

"He makes it clear that in spite of their power, these secret centers of control are seldom in dictatorial positions where they can actually take direct, decisive political action; but their financial stranglehold on the world allows them to *influence and manipulate* the affairs of various nations to an amazing degree and to suit their own purposes. Therefore, whatever the purposes and goals of this group happen to be, they are of monumental importance to the rest of the world."[52]

So the men who control the purse strings, the private international banking cartel, controls the puppet strings of politicians and governments worldwide.

## Gold-Backed Money Disappears

Before we pull back the curtain on some of the players involved in this banking cartel, I want to mention a couple of other important milestones

---

51. *The Naked Capitalist* by W. Cleon Skousen, including excerpts from *Tragedy and Hope* by Carroll Quigley, p. 51-52.
52. Ibid., p. 324.

in monetary system history that led to what is in my opinion, the confiscation of gold.

Our money used to be backed by gold; it was not just paper. It had real value via the value of the gold that backed it. However, that is no longer the case.

This means the paper and coins we now use for buying and selling are fake or faux. They have no intrinsic value; they only have value to the extent of the faith that the public has placed in them. In other words, if everyone woke up tomorrow and realized the "fiat" money was worth nothing and stopped using it, the value *would* be nothing, which is what it really is.

Murray N. Rothbard, author of *The Case Against the Fed*, steps through the road to the fiat money system:

> The other major monetary change accomplished by the New Deal, of course, and done under cover of a depression 'emergency' in the fractional reserve banking system, was to go off the gold standard. After 1933, Federal Reserve notes and deposits were no longer redeemable in gold coins to Americans; and after 1971, the dollar was no longer redeemable in gold bullion to foreign governments and central banks. The gold of Americans confiscated and exchanged for Federal Reserve Notes, which became legal tender; and Americans were stuck in a regime of fiat paper issued by the government and the Federal Reserve... since 1980, the Federal Reserve has enjoyed the absolute power to do literally anything it wants...there are no restraints left on the Federal Reserve. The Fed is the master of all it surveys.[53]

Fiat currencies are not limited to the U.S. Most currencies in the world today are fiat money, such as the euro, the Japanese yen, and the British

---

53. *The Case Against the Fed* by Murray N. Rothbard. Ludwig von Mises Institute, Auburn, AL, 1994, p. 132.

pound. One of my questions is this: Where is all of the gold and silver that used to back these currencies?

The reasons touted for fiat currency were flexibility; ability to adjust them during changing economic conditions; supposed stability; and ease of use.

If there is nothing of tangible worth backing the money, it becomes easier for the Fed to control the perceived value and availability of the money they create and pump out to the public. This fact will be important when the banking elite start to move us into a digital money or token system; we will discuss this shortly.

Rothbard sums up the Federal Reserve System by stating they are accountable to no one; they have no budget, and are never subject to an audit. Yet they are in total control of our money system.

## Those Who Run the Banking System, Run the World

When we talk about those who run the world, many times we refer to them as the elite, the establishment, or the globalists, but who are we really talking about? Does it only go as deep as the richest families in the world? I have to be honest and say *I do not know; everything I read and hear is third hand, and although you can verify sources, can anyone prove who is behind all of this?*

I would say, "No." However, this does not mean you cannot create a rough sketch of the primary players. The bottom line is this: The one thing I can be sure of is that the ultimate power behind the cast of characters in the stage show is a dark power, led by none other than Satan. These characters are part of an overall dark plan, but ultimately the endgame is the same. Whether we are talking about Rothschilds, banking cartels, Council on Foreign Relations, or the pandemic—in my opinion—all roads lead to a Satanic plan to pervert the almighty God's original plan.

Some players include: bankers, the banking cartel, and those who have control of the monetary system. They supersede the governments because in most cases they control the governments worldwide by paying them off to pass legislation that in turn, funds their end game—making more money. That fact leads to more power and control to fund their dark projects.

Skousen explained how the banking cartel was started in Europe by the Rothschild family. "The names of some of these other banking families are familiar to all of us and should be more so. They include Baring, Lazard, Erlanger, Warburg, Schroder, Seligman, the Speyers, Mirabaud, Mallet Fould, and above all Rothschild and Morgan."[54]

He continues describing how many of the banking families in England made their way to the United States to join forces with the American banking dynasties:

"By the beginning of the twentieth century, the American economy had become too dynamic that the major banking dynasties found it increasingly difficult to maintain a tight control. Even the control they had so carefully kept secret was being challenged as a major political issue in national elections."[55]

This group of elite families and world leaders has been working for decades to build what they call a New World Order, a one-world government where everyone and everything is tracked and controlled. Author and radio host Sheila Zilinsky, in her book *Green Gospel: The New World Religion*, makes mention of these groups and discloses a quote by David Rockefeller, who was one of the leading globalists of our time:

---

54. *The Naked Capitalist* by W. Cleon Skousen, including excerpts from *Tragedy and Hope* by Carroll Quigley, Verity Publishing, 1970. The subheadings are by Cleon Skousen, p. 51-52.
55. Ibid.

The New World Order's tentacles reach across the oceans to America, Europe, and the rest of the world with strong connections to the European Royal Families, the Rothschilds, the Pilgrims Society, the Royal Institute of International Affairs, the Bank of England, selected banking and financial institutions … evil Luciferians control their counterparts, including the Rockefellers, the Council on Foreign Relations, the Trilateral Commission, the Bilderberg Group, and the Federal Reserve Bank, among others.

Consider what unashamed predatory globalist David Rockefeller said in his book:

'Some even believe we (the Rockefeller family) are part of a secret cabal working against the best interests of the United states, characterizing my family and me as "internationalists" and of conspiring with others around the world to build a more integrated global political and economic structure—one world, if you will. If that's the charge, I stand guilty, and I am proud of it.'[56]

The Fed is owned by the most affluent people in the world and has been propped up as a government arm to give the appearance of a federally run governmental system.

Although we know the names of some of the elite families, groups, world leaders, and big corporations, this effort started so long ago that the names and faces have changed over time.

The bottom line is that this concept goes back to the spiritual war I have been talking about and will talk about throughout this book. The important thing is that you understand the underpinnings of the banking and governmental foundation so that you understand how it affects your country and ultimately your life.

---

56. Sheila Zilinsky, *Green Gospel: The New World Religion* (Redemption Press, 2015), p. 104.

# Cryptocurrency, Digital Money, Cashless Society, and Control

The primary vehicle that allows us to be free on a daily basis is the ability to buy, sell, and control how we make our money and what we do with our money. If the agenda of a global group of elites is to control the people and their activities, they will most definitely have to control our means to buy and sell, namely our money.

Bitcoin, the first well-known digital money, was introduced to the public around 2009. It was going to be the savior for the little people. It operated outside of a central bank system. There was a finite amount of bitcoin, and all transactions were on a multi-distributed, uncontrolled ledger on blockchain technology that basically kept it out of the hands of any "one" entity, keeping it a free system. This sounded great. I started to study it based on this fact alone.

As time passed, I began to wonder how much of this story was true. Especially when the mainstream media was painting crypto as a bad thing because it was a safe haven for money laundering by drug dealers and other crooks, as if they didn't already exist in the dinosaur fiat money system.

# The Federal Reserve's Central Bank Currency (CBDC)

The Federal Reserve has been discussing the creation of a new, digital fiat currency to be issued by the central banking system and calls it Central Bank Digital Currency (CBDC). Several other countries have already launched their own version of this digital currency or are testing it. The Bahamas was the first country to launch a digital currency in 2020. China has been testing its digital currency, called the Digital Currency Electronic Payment (DCEP), since 2020, and has already begun rolling it out in some cities. Other countries actively developing digital currencies include Sweden, Canada, the United Kingdom, and the European Union.

As I mentioned earlier, bitcoin, and cryptocurrencies in general were created to operate in a decentralized environment, rather than a 'centralized' controlled system such as the Fed. The system would have given people freedom over their money. I believe the central bankers are afraid of this freedom. They want to control the people's money. In my opinion, this is why they demonized bitcoin and other cryptocurrencies.

The Federal Reserve claims their CBDCs will be a secure and efficient way to make payments and purchases. CBDCs are not meant to be an investment asset, but will be a form of digital cash that is under the control of the central bank system. They claim that the benefits of this new digital currency will be efficiency, financial inclusion (giving the 'unbanked' the ability to have access to the currency), improved monetary policy, and reduced fraud and criminal activity, such as counterfeiting, money laundering, and drug dealing.

Again, I don't believe this rubbish. I believe it is about controlling people's money from tracking where they get it to how they use it. So much for privacy. Obviously, regardless of what they say, it will be vulnerable to cyber attacks, data breaches, and ultimately financial losses. If it is digital air, how do you ever get it back?

Catherine Austin Fitts, investment banker and former U.S. Assistant Secretary of Housing during the Bush administration, has said in interviews that she believes bitcoin and other cryptocurrencies were introduced to be the precursor for the Federal Reserve's Central Bank Digital Currency (CBDC)—in other words, what we were told about bitcoin and how it came about was probably another fabricated story.

According to Fitts, giving all control to those that run the world through a central bank digital currency will be the catalyst to end all freedom worldwide:

Without a national sovereignty, you are going to lose individual sovereignty. So this war is going to come down to individual and national sovereignty and with it, can the central bankers implement taxation without representation? And of course their way to do it is to end currency with their currency CBDC; but it's not a currency, it's a control grid. It's a control grid that will permit them to run things centrally with AI and software, and to tax without representation. And if they get their way, they will not only destroy national sovereignty, but destroy all individual sovereignty.[57]

As it stands now, the preliminary CBDC infrastructure is set to launch soon. According to a *Lifesite* article, the Federal Reserve announced a launch of what it calls FedNow. This is a plan that enables all U.S. banks to offer instant payments services, "by linking each banking node directly to the Federal Reserve, according to financial experts."[58]

Time will tell the ultimate outcome, but it appears that the same old storyline is unfolding. The power elite want to control the entire money system, including all details down to every penny people have. In my opinion, this is the beginning of the total control they will have over who gets what money, when they get it, and in some cases whether they get it, based on an individual's 'agreeable' speech or actions.

---

57. Documentary film: "State of Control," directed by Benjamin Jonas Van Den Brink, Quote by Catherine Austin Fitts, Debunk Productions 2022, www.debunkproductions.com.

58. LifesiteNews.com; Federal Reserve announces July launch of central bank digital currency infrastructure, by Emily Mangiaracina, Mar 17, 2023; https://www.lifesitenews.com/news/federal-reserve-announces -july-launch-of-central-bank-digital-currency-infrastructure/.

CHAPTER 4

# Children: Mental, Physical and Spiritual Abuse

## Because it's for the Children

Before the Covid-19 pandemic, who would have guessed everyone would be quarantined in their homes across the nation and the world. "Shelter in place," we were told in order to save lives.

We constantly hear how we need to do something about climate change, gun control, vaccines, and more because it's for the children—we're told—and to save lives.

When I look around our world and the state it is in—death and destruction everywhere—this attitude seems to be hypocritical and backward.

What do I mean? While we had to stay in our homes to "save lives," the Democrat party leaders insisted that Planned Parenthood's abortion clinics stay open to perform abortions. They were determined to keep these death mills open and they wanted funding for these abortion centers included in emergency legislation that was originally created to supposedly help the millions of American people under financial duress after losing their jobs during this pandemic.

How did we get from helping people in an economic emergency to providing more funding for the killing of unborn babies and in some states, killing those who have already been born?

During the quarantine, I had been considering the idea of adopting a pet—a cat from one of our local shelters. So of course, I began searching online to see what cats might be up for adoption in my local area. How eye-opening it was for me when on the homepage of our local Humane Society I read the headline, "Every life counts. As a no-kill shelter, we pride ourselves on providing a sanctuary for animals in need."

Did you get that? "Every life counts ..."

Does it make sense that during a pandemic we need to end the lives of unborn human children when the Humane Society has enough wisdom to say, "Every life counts" when it comes to animal lives? Do people *not* see how ridiculous, horrific, and ironic this is? It should not matter what political party you identify with. This should be obvious to anyone.

Animals' lives are precious, but our own society had sunk so low and become so depraved that while many claimed to care about saving human lives from the Coronavirus at the same time, they wanted to continue ending the lives of innocent, helpless, unborn babies.

What confuses me is that the same people who use "the children" as the reason to get liberal policies into place (gun laws, environmental laws, etc.), they seem to also be the same people who have no problem with the Planned Parenthood agenda to prematurely end lives of human babies.

I am weary of hearing how *everything is for the children*, when on the other hand many states allow the daily murder of nearly 3,000 unborn babies. "After a 30-year decline, abortions in the United States rose by nearly 8% from 2017 to 2020, according to new data from abortion rights group Guttmacher Institute. In 2020, there were 930,160 abortions in the U.S., up from 862,320 abortions in 2017..."[59]

If you believe this is a woman's choice, how is it that *you* were given

59. USA Today; Abortions in the US have increased for the first time in 30 years, new survey finds, by Cady Stanton, Jun 15, 2022; https://www.usatoday.com/story/news/health/2022/06/15/us-abortion-rate-increased-guttmacher/7633229001

the chance to live and yet you are sentencing other potential lives to death prematurely?

There are those who pontificate the following ideas:

"We have to pass the New Green Deal to save the earth and the environment. It's for the children."

"We have to force vaccinate children to keep them in good health. It's for the children."

"We have to pass gun laws to keep schools safe from shootings. It's for the children."

The "It's for the children" mantra is hypocritical. Be honest! How can one believe that killing a baby in the womb is fine, but then claim to care about the welfare of young children? These same people often say it is a woman's right to choose, to abort a baby's life.

Abortion, in my opinion, is the antithesis of the arguments people use to substantiate the agenda items I listed above.

In my opinion, one cannot logically say they care for the children and then agree that babies be aborted when they are inconvenient.

## Baby Kitties and Puppies and Marching in the Streets

Roe v. Wade was enacted fifty-plus years ago and nearly 70 million babies have been killed since then. Who can be proud of that?

In my opinion, if average Americans who believe in the procedure were required to witness an abortion, they would change their minds about this criminal act.

In fact, getting back to my humane society example, I have often said that if these exact procedures were performed on baby kitties and puppies, people would be marching in the streets, calling "Animal cruelty." But these same individuals think it is fine to abort human babies saying, "It's my body."

Author Marnie Pehrson Koons makes a logical argument in her book, *Restoring Liberty: Personal Freedom and Responsibility in America*—and states the following: "We seem to have conflicting laws. Roe v. Wade (not actually a law but a case ruling) said that a mother has a right to abort her child. Yet, if someone murders a pregnant woman and the baby dies, the murderer is convicted of a double homicide."[60]

This doesn't make sense if you truly believe a baby in the womb is *not* yet a person. Why would it be considered double murder by some third party and yet not considered murder by an abortionist doctor and the mother, as the baby is being torn from the womb for the specific purpose of terminating the possibility of having life outside of the womb? The result is the same—death of a baby in the womb.

In my opinion, killing a baby should *not* be a partisan subject. In other words, I am sure there are people on both sides politically who don't believe in abortion; on the flip side, I am sure there are people on both sides politically who may believe abortion is fine. However, sadly, it seems the majority who accept abortion procedures as being fine do lean left politically.

This is a spiritual issue and has dire ramifications for our nation, both spiritually and societally. I believe we are now starting to reap what we have sown for nearly fifty years since passage of the case ruling in 1973.

I feel that Roe v. Wade, although a politically-motivated decision, has made people slowly believe over the decades that it is not only lawful to kill unborn babies, but it is fine if the birth of a baby would pose an inconvenience.

Ironically, this has subconsciously started to break down peoples' belief that the purposeful action of ending someone's life (such as babies in Roe

---

60. Marnie Pehrson Koons, *Restoring Liberty: Personal Freedom and Responsibility in America* (Spirit Tree Publishing, 2018), p 29.

v. Wade), may now be slowly seeping into the belief it is also okay to end an elderly person's life because it will keep him or her from discomfort and/or by the way, since he is old, he doesn't have a reason to keep living. You see where this goes?

It starts to seep into other areas of life. Where do we as a society draw the line when it comes to ending a human life regardless of the age? Do we then say it is now okay to end the life of an autistic or Down's syndrome child? Life is *not* something that should be dictated by others—the Creator God already addressed this in the Second Commandment.

The Tenth Amendment basically states that powers not given to the United States federal government automatically go to the states or the people. Koons also makes the case that matters of murder or wrongful death are rightfully handled by states via the U.S. Constitution.

Koons continues, "So, according to the Constitution, abortion actually would fall under the jurisdiction of the states or the people … decisions about abortion could be handled on a state level or perhaps even on a case-by-case basis like murder trials."[61]

Judeo-Christian values based on the Bible and the Ten Commandments say, "Thou shalt not kill." There is no exception for a baby who is an inconvenient accident for which you can't or don't want to provide care. Adoption is available, and many people who cannot have children consider adoption every day.

## The Color of Abortion

In 2013, I interviewed pastor, author, talk radio host, and founder of the Brotherhood Organization of a New Destiny (BOND), Jesse Lee Peterson, about his book *SCAM: How the Black Leadership Exploits Black America*. While doing research for the program, I learned that nearly 1,900

---

61. Marnie Pehrson Koons, *Restoring Liberty: Personal Freedom and Responsibility in America* (Spirit Tree Publishing, 2018), p 29.

black American babies are aborted daily. I was astounded that this fact is not talked about very much—why aren't black Americans and Black Lives Matter talking about this?

Here is the exchange I had with Jesse Lee as he answered this question:

Angeline: I was using your book and other sources to prepare for this interview today, and I was shocked to find out that the leading cause of death in the black community is abortion. I read averaging from about 1,800 to 1,900 babies a day, more than the white or Hispanic babies. So how can black Americans really believe that the Democratic party has their own best interest in mind? I mean, if they're promoting the genocide against their own race under the guise of a woman's right to choose, why do you think black Americans haven't woken up to that fact yet?

Jesse Lee: Well, first of all, most black people don't see information. They don't go looking for information for themselves. They believe whatever the liberal media and their leaders give them, whatever they say, they fall for it because of the anger of their hearts. And so they don't know. A lot of black people don't even know that every day over 1,800 black babies are being aborted. They are not aware of that, even though there are 70 percent of Planned Parenthood abortion mills within the inner cities around the country—70 percent of them.

But they have been told that those abortion mills are there for healthcare reasons. It's for minorities that can't afford healthcare. And so Planned Parenthood is providing that—that is absolutely not true! But that's what the people are being told. And so they fall for that. I've often said that you can't even be a Christian and support the Democratic platform because the Democratic platform is anti-God, anti-family, anti-freedom, anti-capitalism, anti-anything that's good…they (black community) are absolutely convinced that the Democratic party cares for them and that they'll take care of them and blacks don't have to worry.

It's not true, but they believe that because they're taking the words of someone else rather than looking and understanding for themselves.[62]

Peterson addresses another irony regarding the killing of black babies and the founder of Planned Parenthood, Margaret Sanger, in his book, *From Rage to Responsibility*.

He discusses how Sanger was a eugenicist racist, and that the reason she created Planned Parenthood was not to help unwed mothers who had become pregnant, but that these centers were designed specifically to target and kill the people she thought were inferior in society. Black Americans were in that group of people.

"In Sanger's view, 'Negroes and Southern Europeans,' as she put it, were simply 'mentally inferior to native born Americans,' and minorities in general—including Jewish people—were 'feeble minded,' 'human weeds,' and 'a menace to society.'"

'Blacks ... are a menace to the race,' she once wrote."[63]

It saddens me that black Americans do not know the true history of Planned Parenthood and its founder and how to this day, in my opinion, they are still falling prey to this insidious death cult.

Before I go further, I think defining eugenicist is important because, I believe the eugenics movement is simply the prelude to another movement growing today, *transhumanism* (which I discuss later in this book). I believe transhumanism is an updated form of the eugenics movement of

62. Episode 9 - Truth Seekers Radio Show, Guest: Jesse Lee Peterson-SCAM: How the Black Leadership Exploits Black America, August 2013, https://www.talkshoe.com/recording/inline/key/09f1232e7d4e0ec84a9295d2227a4a4ff348d892.mp3.

63. Margaret Sanger, *Birth Control Review,* April 1933, quoted in Jesse Lee Peterson, *From Rage to Responsibility* (St. Paul, MN, Paragon House, 2000), p. 71.

the 1920s.

Dictionary.com defines eugenics as: "the study of or belief in the possibility of improving the qualities of the human species or a human population, especially by such means as discouraging reproduction by people presumed to have inheritable undesirable traits (negative eugenics) or encouraging reproduction by people presumed to have inheritable desirable traits."[64]

Eugenics is a school of thought that believes society can take measures to remove and replace selected groups of people they deem lesser than with an overall goal of only having a superior race or group of people. As I mentioned earlier, Sanger started Planned Parenthood specifically to remove, or abort, unborn babies of those she believed were the less desirables of her day. Her intentions were anything but philanthropic.

Paul McGuire, speaker and author of the book, *Mass Awakening*, clearly states the early roots of eugenics, including the people and sinister ideas behind the movement.

One of those people, who was instrumental in the eugenics movement, was Bertrand Russell, a British philosopher and intellectual of his day. According to a Wikipedia entry, he is described as having the telltale traits of a eugenicist,

"Early in his life Russell supported eugenicist policies. He proposed in 1894 that the state issue certificates of health to prospective parents and withhold public benefits from those considered unfit. In 1929 he wrote that people deemed 'mentally defective' and 'feebleminded' should be sexually sterilized because they 'are apt to have enormous numbers of illegitimate children, all, as a rule, wholly useless to the community.' Russell was also an advocate of population control."[65]

McGuire writes that Russell was a socialist and atheist who called for

---

64. Dictionary.com, eugenics, https://www.dictionary.com/browse/eugenics.

65. Wikipedia.org, Bertrand Russell, https://en.wikipedia.org/wiki/Bertrand_Russell.

the science of eugenics to be used to create a master race and a slave race, and down to radical ideas such as selective breeding. "Lord Bertrand Russell elaborated, 'Gradually, by selective breeding, the congenital differences between rulers and ruled will increase until they become almost different species… .'"[66]

McGuire reveals that Russell was a New World Order one world government supporter. "Bertrand Russell wrote, 'A scientific world society cannot be stable unless there is a world government.' … Russell called for universal birth control; regular wars and mass starvation are the elites' way to bring about this one world order."[67]

He mentions some others behind the movement one hundred years ago. "The ideas of selective breeding and the science of eugenics were developed with Rockefeller money back in the 1920s. The founder of Planned Parenthood, Margaret Sanger, believed that there were inferior races, and that is why Sanger placed a much higher percentage of abortion clinics in minority neighborhoods."[68]

## Where Will It End?

Some state abortion laws have been continuously relaxed. What do I mean? Originally, abortion was legal only in the first trimester due to Roe v. Wade in 1973. It is also important to note that in 1974 under the National Science Foundation Act, federally-funded research using fetal tissue was prohibited.

The following quotes from the Kaiser Family Foundation show how abortion laws are continuing to expand in some states: "Fast-forward to 2019, New York and Virginia took steps to allow not only late-term abortion, but full-term abortion in some cases. In 2016, Kaiser Family

66. Paul McGuire, *Mass Awakening*, (M House Publishers, Los Angeles, CA, 2015), p. 32.
67. Ibid.
68. Ibid.

Foundation reported that New York state already ranked at the top of all 50 states in the number of abortions performed."[69]

"The new law allows abortion under any of the three conditions: (1) if it is performed earlier than 24 weeks of pregnancy (2) in an absence of fetal viability (3) if necessary to protect the patient's life or health."[70]

So we started from one end of the spectrum in 1973—allowing abortions only during the first trimester, to the other end of the spectrum—allowing abortions even at full-term in some cases. The New York law does not overtly say you can end a baby's life, but the language was left wide open to interpretation.

## The Wasting Away and Depravity of the Public Education System

Aside from the murder of our children, I believe another way we are destroying our nation's children is through the public education system. Although education budgets have continually climbed, it appears that children's performance in areas such as reading are failing.

Here is a summary of approximate total amounts of money spent toward the public education system in the U.S. for the time period ranging from 1950 through 2020:

1950: $12 billion
1970: $107 billion
1990: $342 billion
2010: $1.1 trillion
2020: $1.3 trillion
*Source: National Center for Education Statistics (NCES)

---

69. KFF.org, Kaiser Family Foundation, Rate of Legal Abortions per 1,000 Women Aged 15-44 Years by State of Occurrence.
70. Ibid.

Additionally, statistics from the Literacy Project are not very encouraging:

57 percent of students failed the California Standards Test in English.

1/3 of fourth graders reach the proficient reading level.

25 percent of students in California school systems are able to perform basic reading skills.

85 percent of juvenile offenders have problems reading.

65 percent of America's fourth graders do not read at a proficient level.[71]

In May 2023, an online article regarding child illiteracy in America published by Regis College reveals these sad statistics:

"Some 34 percent of students are below basic reading level in the fourth grade, according to the U.S. National Center for Education Statistics (NCES). Another 31 percent are below the proficient reading level … 27 percent of eighth grade students are below basic reading level, per NCES. Another 39 percent are below the proficient reading level."[72]

So why are our children failing miserably in all areas of education while we continue throwing more and more money at the public education system?

This is *not* at all by accident, but is being done intentionally for a multitude of reasons that lead us back to the control I've discussed in this book. A less intelligent and critical-thinking population is easier to control. It seems that school-aged children's curricula are more about brainwashing them in social justice ideas and less concerned about teaching them reading, writing, and mathematics skills.

---

71. LiteracyProject.org, 30 Key Child Literacy Stats Parents Need to be Aware Of, February 14, 2019, by admin-travis https://literacyproj.org/2019/02/14/30-key-child-literacy-stats-parents-need-to-be-aware-of/.

72. Regis College, Child Illiteracy in America: Statistics, Facts, and Resources, September 28, 2021, https://online.regiscollege.edu/blog/child-illiteracy/.

Political commentator and author Ann Coulter drives home this point in her book, *Godless*:

"It's very important for the Democrats to control the public schools. John Dewey, the founder of public education in America, said, 'You can't make socialists out of individualists—children who know how to think for themselves spoil the harmony of the collective society, which is coming, where everyone is interdependent.' You also can't make socialists out of people who can read, which is probably why Democrats think the public schools have nearly achieved Aristotelian perfection."[73]

Coulter gives an example of throwing more money after bad to fix the so-called 'failing education system':

> Between 1982 and 2001, spending on New York City public schools increased by more than 300 percent, ... New York State courts officially found in 2003 that graduates of New York City's public schools were not competent to sit on a jury ... the courts found that schools were not providing children with such skills as 'basic literacy, calculating and verbal skills necessary to enable children to eventually function productively as civil participants capable of voting and serving on a jury.' In response, the courts ordered that yet more money be spent on the same failing public schools.[74]

Coulter wrote this back in 2006 before the disaster we know as public education included radical ideas such as: social justice, gender fluidity, and Critical Race Theory (CRT). It is my belief, the curricula aims to brainwash young people into hating the United States, American history, and anyone who is Caucasian.

The nightmare seems to place more emphasis on dragging students down to the lowest levels of moral depravity by telling boys they can be

---

73. Ann Coulter, *Godless* (New York, Crown Forum, 2006), p 152.
74. Ibid., p 163.

girls, or girls they can be boys, or better yet, they can be anything they want, including an animal, and changes can be made any day of the week.

## Teaching Gender Confusion

I remember being an adolescent. It was an awkward time of life as hormones and physical body changes took place. I cannot imagine someone telling me as a pre-teen that I might feel better being a boy, and that this would be the solution to my lack of self-confidence. Teaching young people these evil and perverted ideas is setting them up for a lifetime of destruction.

In an interview I conducted with Dr. Karen Siegemund, president of American Freedom Alliance, she said that if a child in school identifies as a gender that is the opposite gender than he or she was born with, and his or her teacher or classmates don't refer to him or her as they request, there can be penalties for being disrespectful to this trans person. [75]

Where did this gender propaganda wave originate?

Gender dysphoria has exploded. In 2013, there were only three clinics in the United States that catered to these transgender cases. When I did research in 2019, there were more than forty-one clinics nationally, and they reported a 400 percent increase in children and teens who now identify as transgender. *The Western Journal* reported a sharp increase in the number of clinics as of October 2022, "…Society for Evidence Based Gender Medicine estimates over 300."[76]

Now I ask you, where in the world are these children and young people getting this idea that they are transgender? It's almost becoming the trendy thing to do.

---

75. Episode 69 - Truth Seekers Radio Show, Guest: Dr. Karen Siegmund from the American Freedom Alliance, https://www.talkshoe.com/recording/inline/key/3cd007a23dddf6b188cfbbbfedc2234c55b9093c.mp3.

76. *The Western Journal*, Number of Pediatric 'Gender Clinics' Exploding Across the Country, by Laurel Duggan, October 2022, https://www.westernjournal.com/number-pediatric-gender-clinics-exploding-across-country/.

According to a 2022 *New York Times* article, the numbers continue to rise: "The number of young people who identify as transgender has nearly doubled in recent years, according to a new report that captures a stark generational shift and emerging societal embrace of a diversity of gender identities."[77]

"Experts said that young people increasingly have the language and social acceptance to explore their gender identities, whereas older adults may feel more constrained. But the numbers, which vary widely from state to state, also raise questions about the role of peer influence or the political climate of the community."[78]

Notice the *experts* say it may have to do with peer influence or the political climate of the community; however, they neglect to mention the influence of public schools and colleges in this equation. I believe the education system, the media, Big Pharma, and the healthcare system play the biggest roles in this perversion.

Research published by Grand View Research and reported by the DailyWire.com stated, gender transition is growing into a lucrative business sector:

"The industry surrounding transgender surgeries is expected to reach $5 billion by the end of the decade. According to a recent report from Grand View Research, the sector saw a $1.9 billion valuation last year and is forecast to expand at a compound annual growth rate of more than 11% through 2030. 'The rising incidences of gender dysphoria and the increasing number of people opting for gender confirmation surgeries are expected to boost the growth during the forecast period,' the analysis

---

77. *New York Times*, "Report Reveals Sharp Rise in Transgender Young People in the U.S." by Azeen Ghorayshi, June 10, 2022, https://www.nytimes.com/2022/06/10/science/transgender-teenagers-national-survey.html.
78. Ibid.

explained."[79]

This annual steady growth increase in my estimation only fuels this fire in terms of encouraging and cultivating this lucrative niche for Big Pharma and healthcare providers. And how is it that such a high percentage are boys seven years old on average? Where did this gender dysphoria come from overnight? I am not saying there may not be some genuine isolated cases, but I think it is pretty coincidental that these numbers seem to skyrocket in tandem with the intense push by the media and educational systems.

As if these ideas will not cause enough damage, colleges, schools, and even lawmakers are starting to force their perversion into the language. If you use, write, or speak the wrong pronoun, you may have to pay a heavy price in fines or even jail time.

## Perversion of Words and the Destruction of Pronouns

You will see there is an obvious, deliberate perversion of our language if you listen to many types of media, especially in mainstream news or culture. I believe they are trying to censor our speech by changing the meanings of words. The destruction of our traditional English pronouns are under attack as they try to invent a new, more inclusive type. Now people who use traditional pronouns are getting fined for using what many consider proper English grammar.

Here is the text from a short clip of an exchange I had with radio host, Tom Donahue, on an episode of the *Tom Donahue Show*:

Angeline: "There was a case in Canada where a minister got in trouble for calling a transgender woman who used to be a man, a him, I think, and he got fined for calling him a him. You cannot use he and she, instead

---

79. DailyWire.com, Transgender Surgery Poised to Become a $5Billion Industry, by Ben Zeisloft, Oct. 2022, https://www.dailywire.com/news/transgender-surgery-poised-to-become-a-5-billion-industry.

you use the word Ze, like the letter Z-E—I guess that's the old he. And then the new her is Z-I-R , Zir—Ze and Zir. Those are the politically correct pronouns that you can use. "

Tom: "The Progressive left does not even want to use male or female, it has to be unisex."[80]

They are trying to pervert our speech. How are they doing this? In the case of proper pronouns, they have a newly manufactured set of pronouns created for LGBTQ language that is created for what they call the non-binary set of people.

From what I can tell in my research, non-binary means a population that does not subscribe to any particular typical gender type, such as a male or female. So these are the new pronouns that they're allowing us to use—yes, I said—*allowing* us.

This becomes more ridiculous as you look into it. I got so confused I stopped looking.

So why am I talking about this? Because they are deliberately perverting language everywhere and no one is stopping them.

## Forced Perversion

Whether you are willing to acknowledge this perversion of gender or not, many of our societal institutions are ramming it through at full speed.

We discussed education's pivotal role in this, but even the American Psychiatric Association that once classified transgender behavior as a mental disorder changed their position in 2012. They reclassified it to gender dysphoria, meaning that it is a condition of having emotional distress related to one's gender identity, but is no longer a mental disorder.[81] It has

---

80. Tom Donahue Reports, LGBTQ, Language, Identity Bias and PC Trans-World Changes, Episode 9, https://player.fm/series/tom-donahue-reports/tom-donahue-show-week-9
81. National Institute of Corrections, Being transgender no longer a "mental disorder": APA (2012) https://nicic.gov/weblink/being-transgender-no-longer-mental-disorder-apa-2012.

now been accepted as mainstream behavior. Maybe not to you or me, but trust me, within one generation it will be *normalized.*

The research I conducted in 2019 showed that 75 to 95 percent of children who go through puberty and don't get transgender treatment end up being comfortable in their bodies as time goes on. So 75 to 95 percent of kids that are confused when they're young get over the confusion.

What about those who undergo a gender transformation?

The *New York Post* published an article about a study in Sweden that shows adults who went through this sex reassignment surgery are nineteen times more likely to commit suicide.[82]

So there's the information that you never hear about. You never hear about the consequences of this surgery. The study stated that the long-term effects of altering children's hormones are unknown.

Advocates appear to treat this serious matter as a child or young person's choice that should be made without interference or advice.

I believe this movement is evil and is an intentional perversion of God's creation; it is trying to destroy the image of man—as God created man and woman in His image. This is the spiritual side of the warfare. In the physical realm, dire consequences could result for these individuals; only time will tell.

The educational, media, and healthcare institutions are at the foundation of this movement, and the children and most parents don't realize what's happening. They think it's a trend and don't recognize that this insidious plan could destroy lives.

The devil, on the other hand, knows exactly what is being done, as he is the orchestrator of the movement, in my opinion.

John 10:10 says, "The thief cometh not, but for to steal, kill, and to *destroy.*"

---

82. NYPost.com, Parents speak out about the "rush" to reassign the gender of their kids, by Jane Ridley, June 30, 2021 https://nypost.com/2021/06/30/inside-the-rush-to-reassign-the-genders-of-kids/.

# CHAPTER 5

# Hollywood and the Media

*(how you're being propagandized)*

## Theatre Diabolique

Many times as I reflect on what is transpiring in our world, day after day, it almost seems unreal. Every day seems to bring more evil or ridiculous happenings than the day before. My mother and I always say, "When you think you've seen and heard it all—something worse appears on the news the next day."

When I contemplate these almost surreal happenings, I picture it as what I've come to call, "Theatre Diabolique," translated to mean the "Devil's Stage." *Webster's New Collegiate Dictionary* defines diabolical (the English form of the French term, *diabolique*) as "relating to or characteristic of the devil; fiendish."[83]

I see these happenings as so evil that we aren't just experiencing them as a natural unfolding of events, but as a "supernatural" orchestration playing out in events as a way of controlling our behavior and environment.

So let's go back to the question I posed earlier, "How do you know what you know?" Most of what we experience through the media, in my opinion, is created through productions to give us the illusion of reality. Here is an example:

---

83. *Webster's New Collegiate Dictionary* (G. & C. Merriam Co., 1974), p. 313.

I remember the first time I saw the movie, *Wag the Dog*. In the movie, to distract the public and media from a sex scandal during a presidential election, a war in Albania was manufactured and faked by a film director hired to get attention off of the sex scandal and onto the war.

When I saw this movie, I was convinced that its purpose was to reveal to viewers that Hollywood has the power to manipulate the masses through the manufacturing of the illusions it creates, and that the media and entertainment industries do indeed do this.

## A History of Tinseltown

I interviewed Jay Dyer, author of the book, *Esoteric Hollywood: Sex, Cults and Symbols in Film*. He has studied many forms of film and media and has uncovered what he believes are true insidious and mysterious messages and symbolism disseminated through the Hollywood empire and fed to an unaware public that is seemingly willing to lap it all up.

In his book, Dyer compares ancient Babylon to today's Hollywood on a political and spiritual level and how show business is really used to pump out propaganda. "Babylon was the ancient pagan empire prominent in biblical prophetic works as an enemy of God's people due to their idolatry. Hollywood is no different, functioning as the propaganda arm of the antichrist media establishment, intent on re-engineering society into its alchemical opposite, unleashing destructive forces of cultural Marxism and death."[84]

He goes on to explain how the stages of ancient Greece and Rome were more than dramatic entertainment; they had a sacred spiritual role in society to interact with and worship their gods through ritual on stage. Things have not changed and in our society today, the Hollywood stage has the same role as in ancient societies—but unfortunately, most of the

---

84. Jay Dyer, *Esoteric Hollywood: Sex, Cults and Symbols in Film*, (Trine Day LLC., Walterville, 2016), p. 12.

audience has no idea of the insidious purpose behind the actors and their dramatic roles.

Dyer states, "From its beginnings, Hollywood has been an empire of tragedies, full of lost lives, drugs, and real-life drama, but this troupe life-style is nothing new. The stage has long been the site of tragedy and some-thing much darker—ritual invocation, all the way back to the ancient Greeks and Romans. For Greece and, in debased form, Rome, the stage was sacred where the dramaturgical interactions of the gods were actually a form of magical invocation. The actors donned the costumes of the gods, with the playwright scripting the narrative to inculcate the masses into the appropriate morals of the state. Although the idea of the theater as explicitly sacred is foreign to the modernity, it was not for historic man, nor is modern man's praxis any less religious in regard to theater."[85]

I had heard many claims that the Central Intelligence Agency (CIA) had also been involved in the entertainment industry for decades and that several well-known actors and actresses were CIA operatives. It sounded unbelievable, so when I had the opportunity to interview Dyer regarding Hollywood, I asked him about the connection between intelligence agencies, government, and the entertainment industry.

Dyer admitted that based on his research and study, a relationship between intelligence agencies, government, and the entertainment industry has been the driver behind a type of social engineering in our society—via the pumping out of propaganda. When I asked him if he thought Hollywood had been originally created for this specific purpose, or if government and intelligence agencies just happened to coincidentally find themselves in a perfect setup to use Hollywood assets for their pur-poses—he said he believed it was the former.

His explanation clearly shows that although the U.S. historically

---

85. Ibid.

became independent from England—the tentacles that reached across the pond were still at work trying to influence the American way of life through Hollywood propaganda.

Dyer expanded on the British connection in our radio interview:

> It was always intended to be that way, particularly when you look at the planning of the Royal Society and groups like the Fabian Society at the Tavistock Institute in England. These are British think tanks and social engineering outfits that decided you could utilize moving pictures for the purpose of propaganda. So early on, especially back in the early days of film, twenties and thirties it was done primarily for war propaganda. Some of the earliest stuff is war propaganda and the military saw right away this could be useful for that effect.
>
> You have Germans using cameras to film propaganda; you have this done by the British, and then the decision was made by the Royal Society in London, that rather than locate Hollywood in England, which is sort of the foundation of modern acting and theatre, with the Globe Theatre and Shakespeare; rather the decision was made that it would be Hollywood. That is why you find early on in Hollywood with MGM and these different studios having a direct connection to British intelligence through people like Hitchcock and various British writers like Ian Fleming or Noel Coward or Will Dahl—all these British agents that actually worked for British intelligence were instrumental in shifting and pumping certain policies and films to be made in the Golden and Silver era of Hollywood.[86]

In his book, he dedicated a chapter to this subject called "The CIA and Hollywood—A Dark Marriage," in which he takes a quote from the *Los Angeles Times* that reveals the CIA and the role they play in some

---

86. *The Truth Seekers Radio Show*. Episode 51; Jay Dyer author and radio show host of "Esoteric Hollywood—the dark side of the entertainment industry," 2014.

Hollywood projects.

> The CIA has long had a special relationship with the entertainment industry, devoting considerable attention to fostering relationships with Hollywood movers and shakers, studio executives, producers, directors, big-name actors. John Rizzo, the former acting CIA general counsel, wrote in his new book, *Company Man: Thirty Years of Crisis and Controversy in the CIA...*

> The CIA also recruits actors to give more visibility to propaganda projects abroad, such as a documentary secretly produced by the agency, Rizzo said. And the agency sometimes takes advantage of the door-opening cachet that movie stars and other American celebrities enjoy. A star who met a world leader, for example, might be asked for details about that meeting.

> The CIA has officials assigned full-time to the care and feeding of Hollywood assets, Rizzo wrote. Other former CIA officials added that some of those operatives work in the Los Angeles office of an agency department called the National Resources Division, which recruits people in the U.S. to help America spy abroad.[87]

Hollywood always seems to push the envelope one way or another, but in most recent decades, there has been a big push to what I would describe as a very "dark spiritual side." I see it especially in films and television shows that are the average fare of the day. Hollywood was originally created to set the tone for most everything from pop culture to religion, politics, or anything the establishment wants to be on *top of mind* for the general public through their corporate-owned news and media channels.

Those in charge set the agenda of the day—entertainment and news media carry it out.

---

87. Jay Dyer, *Esoteric Hollywood: Sex, Cults and Symbols in Film,* Trine Day LLC., Walterville, 2016, p. 345.

As far as law enforcement was concerned, I'd always heard the Federal Bureau of Investigation (FBI) was in charge of domestic law enforcement and the Central Intelligence Agency (CIA) was in charge of international affairs.

In recent years as I've researched political subjects both domestic and international, it seems the lines have been blurred. I have to believe those in charge know it and probably use loopholes available to them to use tools they want to get things done no matter the jurisdiction.

In Servando Gonzalez's book, *Psychological Warfare and the New World Order: The Secret War Against the American People*, he mentions a statement by author Ralph W. McGehee, former CIA officer, that alludes to the purpose of the CIA.

Now let me say at the outset that if a CIA officer, current or former, puts out a book, that in and of itself should cause readers to look at such a book with a critical eye.

Here is an excerpt from McGehee's original statement as taken from Gonzalez's book regarding the CIA's effect on American people domestically. "The CIA is not now nor has it ever been a central intelligence agency. It is the covert action arm of the President's foreign policy advisers. In that capacity it overthrows or supports foreign governments while reporting 'intelligence' justifying those activities ... disinformation is a large part of its covert action responsibility, and the American people are the primary target audience of its lies."[88]

So basically the CIA has the role of manipulating and twisting information and then disseminating it to the masses to take it in, chew on it, and ultimately believe it—and they do.

The following quote by Neil Postman, author of *Amusing Ourselves to*

---

88. Servando Gonzalez, *Psychological Warfare and the New World Order: The secret war against the American people* (Oakland, California, Spook Books, 2010), p.26-27.

*Death: Public Discourse in the Age of Show Business,* sums it up perfectly: "Disinformation does not mean false information. It means misleading information—misplaced, irrelevant, fragmented, or superficial information—information that creates the illusion of knowing something, but which in fact leads one away from knowing."[89] —Neil Postman, 1985

Another finger was pointed at the CIA and its relationship with mainstream press and news publishers in 1977 by Watergate scandal reporter Carl Bernstein in a *Rolling Stones Magazine* article called, "The CIA and the Media." He claims this relationship dated back to the early days of the Cold War in the early 1950s. He lists some of these relationships in the article:

> Among the executives who lent their cooperation to the Agency were William Paley of the Columbia Broadcasting System, Henry Luce of Tirne Inc., Arthur Hays Sulzberger of the New York Times, Barry Bingham Sr. of the Louisville Courier-Journal, and James Copley of the Copley News Service. Other organizations which cooperated with the CIA include the American Broadcasting Company, the National Broadcasting Company, the Associated Press, United Press International, Reuters, Hearst Newspapers, Scripps-Howard, Newsweek magazine, the Mutual Broadcasting System, the Miami Herald and the old Saturday Evening Post and New York Herald-Tribune.

> By far the most valuable of these associations, according to CIA officials, have been with the New York Times, CBS, and Time Inc.[90]

My question is: Why would they let him write this article and allow

---

89. Neil Postman, *Amusing Ourselves to Death: Public Discourse in the Age of Show Business* (M Penguin Group/Penguin Books USA Inc., New York 1985).

90. *Rolling Stone* Magazine, Carl Bernstein, The CIA and the Media, 1977. https://www.carlbernstein.com/the-cia-and-the-media-rolling-stone-10-20-1977.

its publication? Would it have anything to do with Postman's quote about putting out misleading information? Could there have been a motive other than the obvious for the publication of this article? In 1977, this story would have been a bombshell, whistle-blower type report.

The more I read and learn about the agency, I don't doubt they interfere and manipulate international affairs and governments to fulfill their missions. It seems they indeed literally play different roles to program the minds of the American people to believe that what they hear and see on the international front is reality—when all along it is part of the fictional made-up drama that is part of the Theatre Diabolique.

## And Now, the News

In the early 1990s when I was still studying journalism, NBC's *Dateline* program was producing a story on older model General Motor trucks they claimed had defective fuel tank designs that could cause fires and/or explosions in car crashes. The report contained films of crash tests that pointed out serious flaws, no doubt to convince the public of the danger. However, GM claimed NBC had gone too far and accused the network of purposely setting up the tests to rig fires on cue for the cameras—giving the appearance of naturally occurring fires in the crash tests.

In my opinion, to impact viewers' minds, the goal was to show fiery crash test results.

Being that this story was just a distant memory, I started to research it again and found many interesting details that had been published in a 1993 report by the *Washington Post*. Keeping in mind that the goal of the crash tests was to show how dangerous the GM trucks could be in a collision scenario, the *Washington Post* reported the following:

"The fuel tank in NBC's crash test did not rupture. The collision produced some dramatic footage—gasoline spraying from the tank's filler neck and igniting—but the fire lasted 15 seconds, went out by itself, and caused almost no damage to the truck."[91]

So according to this report, the "fiery crashes" that were broadcast were *not* a reality, only a theatrical production.

Interestingly, the *Washington Post* goes on to say that *Dateline* reporter Michele Gillen was never onboard to do the crash tests because they had footage from real accident scenes.

Gillen was obviously disturbed by the 'manufactured' portrayal because the report said she called the head of the show and wanted the test discontinued. Let me interject here. This is what an objective journalist with integrity would do.

After the first test failed to cause a big fiery scene, Gillen was told to continue with the tests, and the next test was even more disappointing—no fiery scene for the cameras to film. In fact, according to the *Washington Post* report, the owner of the company that did the tests, Bruce Enz, in an interview, recalled Gillen stating, "Well, the tanks held up ... I doubt whether we can use it."[92]

Although Gillen's concern was significant enough for her to contact the head of the program to try to discontinue the tests, her remark about her doubt of their use since they were unsuccessful could call into question whether she would have looked the other way if the setup tests had been successful. I guess we will never know for sure.

According to the report, here is what was shown to the audience in this Theatre Diabolique:

"But when Dateline aired its segment, the crash tests were not only included, they were presented as the coup de grace. More than 20 million viewers watched a car colliding with a GM truck and heard Gillen describe

---

91. WashingtonPost.com, *Does TV News Go Too Far? A Look Behind the Scenes at NBC's Truck Crash Test* (Washington Post, Feb. 1993).
92. Ibid.

how the spray from the gas tank's filler neck "erupted into flames," ignited by a spark from the headlight. The 56-second segment includes a terrifying scene: a driver's view of the last moments before impact as captured by a camera tied to the steering wheel."[93]

And the report goes on to state what details were hidden from the audience—"Gillen did not say the fire lasted only 15 seconds. She did not say the fire went out on its own. She did not say that *Dateline* had reversed the order of the crashes so that the demonstration culminated in a burst of fire, rather than a dud. She did not say that the gasoline tank's cap was a replacement that might not have properly fit, which could have been the reason it flew off and allowed gasoline to escape."[94]

To their credit, NBC did say, " … The tests were 'unscientific crash demonstrations' and the gas tank had not ruptured. 'If it had, the fire would have been much larger,' Gillen said in the broadcast."[95]

At the end of the day, NBC's credibility was questionable at best and they apologized for the shoddy report after a GM lawsuit pushed the issue.

As far as Michele Gillen's credibility is concerned, I must say this about her. I remember how disappointed I was at the time of the story. I had grown up in the South Florida area and had seen her face and work in the local Miami market for years. She seemed very professional and had a reputation of being a great anchor and reporter—I looked up to her at the time.

I'm not sure how I feel about Gillen's part in this. I know from experience that it can appear she was pulled into a web of deception, especially if her story was edited by someone else at the network. If the *Washington Post* report is accurate (question everything), she did have misgivings about the tests early on.

---

93. Ibid.
94. Ibid.
95. Ibid.

The end of this story brought me back to the time when I did the story on the Christian students' group on my college campus and when my story aired, everything had been juxtaposed and unrecognizable to me.

## Now You See It, Now You Don't

When I heard about a story that broke in October 2019, I couldn't ignore it, and the questions it raises about our media and how they knowingly or unknowingly (tongue in cheek) have the power to manipulate the public with manufactured productions they sell as news stories.

ABC's *News World Tonight* aired a story that showed video news footage about a supposed war that broke out in northern Syria between Turkey and U.S. allied Kurds after Trump pulled American forces out of the area. The problem was that parts of the video news footage they showed were actually shot in 2017 at a Kentucky gun range—quite a long way from Syria.

Several people noticed the resemblances of the video footage between the ABC news footage and the video posted in 2017 from a Kentucky gun range—questions about the story's authenticity arose.

In October 2019, shortly after the ABC report aired, *USA Today* reported the following regarding the video footage debacle: "*ABC News* apologized Monday after airing a video that it originally purported to be a depiction of a Turkish attack in northern Syria against Kurdish civilians after some raised concerns about its similarity to a 2017 video of a Kentucky military gun show. The video first aired on *World News Tonight* on Sunday evening. As the video played, anchor Tom Llamas said it appeared "to show Turkey's military bombing Kurd civilians in a Syrian border town."[96]

---

96. USAToday.com, ABC News Mistakenly Airs Video from Kentucky Gun Show as Syria Bombing Footage (Courier Journal, Oct. 2019), https://www.courier-journal.com/story/news/local/2019/10/15/abc-news-airs-knob-creek-kentucky-gun-range-video-as-syria-bombing/3976328002/.

After the deceptive video footage was aired on ABC's *News World Tonight* and *Good Morning America* programs, and the similarities came to light, the network posted the following apology regarding the mistake on their Twitter account on October 14, 2019: "CORRECTION: We've taken down video that aired on "World News Tonight Sunday" and "Good Morning America" this morning that appeared to be from the Syrian border immediately after questions were raised about its accuracy. ABC News regrets the error."[97]

A *New York Times* article regarding the video footage raised a huge red flag in my mind about whether the news organization knew what they were airing was inauthentic from the beginning. Why do I say this?

Here are two quotes from *ABC News* published by the New York Times report. One quote is from the original ABC report, and the other is a quote that was issued in their apology after the faulty report aired. See if you can find a similar play on words between these two quotes.

The *New York Times* on October 2019 in an article titled, "ABC Apologizes for Showing Video from U.S. Gun Range in Report on Syria," quoted ABC's explanation of the mistake: "We've taken down video that aired on 'World News Tonight Sunday' and 'Good Morning America' this morning that appeared to be from the Syrian border immediately after questions were raised about its accuracy," the network said in a statement on Monday. "ABC News regrets the error."[98]

The *New York Times* continued to state that *ABC News* declined to say how the mistake could have happened. Here is the second quote from *The New York Times* report, taken directly from the original news story as it aired, "Tom Llamas, an anchor with ABC News's "World News Tonight" spoke over the footage, which someone reposted on YouTube. 'This video,

---

97. Ibid.

98. NYTimes.com, ABC Apologizes for Showing Video from U.S. Gun Range in Report on Syria (The New York Times, Oct. 2019).

right here, appearing to show Turkey's military bombing Kurd civilians in a Syrian border town,' Mr. Llamas said."[99]

Did you notice the similar words? The keyword is *appearing*.

The first quote says, "…that appeared to be from the Syrian border …"

*ABC News* said, *appeared*—ABC did not say, "is from the Syrian border."

Since this is the quote issued *after* the story aired, and is supposed to be an apology for the mistaken report, I could see why the statement would use the word *appeared*—meaning it appeared *to look as though* but may not necessarily have been how it appeared.

But what I thought was odd is how the word *appearing* was used *during* the report when it aired live by ABC News. The anchor, Tom Llamas, said, " … *appearing* to show Turkey's military bombing Kurd civilians in a Syrian border town."

Why would Llamas have used the word *appearing* as if it might not necessarily be what was transpiring? I can bet it was written into his news copy script on the teleprompter. But why was it written like that in a story that was supposedly showing "real news" happening?

If I had reported this story and believed the footage was real, I would have said, "Here is footage of Turkey's military on the ground in northern Syria … " I would not think to use the word *appear*.

Could it be that ABC knew the footage was not actual footage shot for this story? I am asking the question because I thought using the words, *appearing* and *appeared* were odd choices if they believed the footage was authentic.

Here is another important point reported in *The New York Times* article that might explain the use of this gun range footage in ABC's story, "The clip that accompanied the reports on the bombings showed explosions

---

99. Ibid.

and smoke dominating the dark horizon."[100]

When you view the footage from the Kentucky gun range, the description above from *The New York Times* article is accurate. The gun range footage shows explosions and smoke in the dark night—it is very intense and has a shocking effect when viewed.

I contend this footage was inserted into the report for just that reason—for effect. Can I prove ABC did this intentionally, thinking they'd never get caught? No. But I am saying that I am not so sure it was a mistake. I lean towards the idea that the news footage editor thought it would make a great, shocking news story with the footage inserted.

To be fair, *The New York Times* article goes on to explain that the vetting of video footage for authenticity can be done through a reverse-imaging search and maybe ABC was short-staffed and under pressure to get the story out.

Here are some questions and observations I reached after researching this story.

#1 - How did they "mistakenly" use footage from a gun range that was already two years old in a report taking place in northern Syria?

#2 - Again, why would the reporter say, "appearing to show" instead of, "This footage shows … "?

#3 - I find it frightening that pre-Internet, this mistake would never have been discovered. It is only because several people saw similar video footage in the ABC report and the gun range footage posted online that called the story into question in the first place.

Think of all of the news stories that aired before the Internet. How many faulty reports were filed?

I thought bringing this story to your attention shows how important

---

100. NYTimes.com, ABC Apologizes for Showing Video from U.S. Gun Range in Report on Syria (*The New York Times*, Oct. 2019).

it is for people to watch news and other media with a critical eye. Don't take everything at face value. You may not be seeing what you think you are seeing after all.

## More Illusions Abound

I remember when I was in my first two years of college studying journalism, we were required to read Neil Postman's *Amusing Ourselves to Death: Public Discourse in the Age of Show Business*. It made an impact on me because even as a young person, I thought about the impact television made on people. I thought life imitated art, or what came out of the "boob tube."

Postman gives an example of how 'top of mind' issues of our day only exist in the world of entertainment and how the gods of the entertainment industry create the script and push it out to the masses to create their *reality*. The only way it can become our reality is if we *accept* it as our reality.

Postman demonstrates this in what he calls, "the news of the day." He says that it simply did not exist in our society until television came into being and created and disseminated it as such.

Postman explains it this way:

> The information, the content, or, if you will, the "stuff" that makes up what is called "the news of the day" did not exist— could not exist—in a world that lacked the media to give it expression. I do not mean that things like fires, wars, murders and love affairs did not, ever and always, happen in places all over the world. I mean that lacking the technology to advertise them, people could not attend to them, could not include them in their daily business. Such information simply could not exist as part of the content of culture. This idea—that there is a content called "the news of the day"—was entirely created by the telegraph (and since amplified by newer media), which made it

possible to move decontextualized information over vast spaces at incredible speed. The news of the day is a figment of our technological imagination. It is, quite precisely, a media event… Cultures without speed-of-light media—let us say, cultures in which smoke signals are the most efficient space-conquering tool available—do not have news of the day. Without a medium to create its form, the news of the day does not exist.[101]

Wow! When I read this, it gelled with an idea I had thought about in 2020 during the 24-7 coverage of the Covid19 pandemic.

When everyone was in lockdown in my area, I would look out the window and everything seemed still and peaceful. The world I saw from my window did not match the world pictured on the television screen. I saw a beautiful blue sky, fluffy white clouds, sunshine, quiet, and peace.

At that moment it hit me that if there were no television, radio, newspaper, or social media, you would never know about the Covid monster out there, ready to take you down at any minute—the monster we saw on television images, the unseen monster that brought people to their death on the streets of China.

As Postman said, I am not denying there was a virus or something that made people ill, and in some cases caused death. But it was not lurking behind every tree if you went outdoors without a mask. If this was the case, all of humanity would be gone by now. This *picture of fear* is the construct of the media—the construct that many people have accepted as their reality.

This construct of fear would have no life if it were not for the media outlets of our day. This is what I believe Postman was trying to illustrate in his "news of the day" example.

If all of this is true, you have a choice whether or not to make the rub-

---

101. Neil Postman, *Amusing Ourselves to Death: Public Discourse in the Age of Show Business* (M Penguin Group/Penguin Books USA Inc., New York 1985), p. 7-8.

bish of the day's headlines your reality. You can decide to invite this fear into your reality or not. If you do, then what kind of life are you living anyway? A life of fear is not living because it paralyzes and enslaves you mentally, physically, emotionally, and spiritually.

Your Creator wanted you to be *free*. You can be free by looking at this truth. So what type of life will you choose? The state of truth and freedom, or the state of fear and enslavement?

## Social Media, the Latest Propaganda Tool

Let me say at the outset of this subject. I don't have, never had, and will never have a Facebook account, either personal or business. I always had a gut feeling there was something sinister about it. I'm not condemning those who have a Facebook account; I am just saying it is *not* for me.

I never bought the Facebook story of Mark Zuckerberg and friends organically coming up with a social app for their college. This same social app caught on like wildfire and has convinced people worldwide to put their entire life on it for the world to see. Counter to the cover story, I suspected that it was a datamining project manufactured by the government to get people to willingly and freely give up their personal data. This was just my opinion.

I have heard about Facebook possibly being a CIA-related project but never looked into these claims. I recently came across an article published on ZDnet.com in 2008 where author Tim Hodgkinson explains findings that show a connection between a Facebook board member and the CIA. Hodgkinson goes much further, digging deep into the background of board member Jim Breyer, asserting that his connections bring Facebook uncomfortably close to the CIA:

"Facebook's most recent round of funding was led by a company called Greylock Venture Capital, who put in the sum of $27.5 million. One of

Greylock's senior partners is called Howard Cox, another former chairman of the NVCA (*National Venture Capital Association*), who is also on the board of In-Q-Tel. What's In-Q-Tel? Well, believe it or not (and check out their website), this is the venture capital wing of the CIA."[102]

Recently while doing research on Facebook and their digital currency plans, I stumbled on information in the press that states a project very similar to Facebook has ties to the government through the Department of Defense.

## Social Media Illusions

While researching Facebook's original digital currency project called Libra, I came across information about LifeLog. This was a planned project from The Defense Advanced Research Projects Agency known as DARPA, an agency under the U.S. Department of Defense according to their Wikipedia entry, " … responsible for the development of emerging technologies for use by the military."[103]

Apparently this agency had plans for a project called LifeLog. It is eerily similar to the Facebook app that people have been using since 2006. According to an article in *Wired*, the LifeLog project was shelved by the Pentagon in 2004:

> The Pentagon canceled its so-called LifeLog project, an ambitious effort to build a database tracking a person's entire existence.
>
> Run by DARPA, the Defense Department's research arm, LifeLog aimed to gather in a single place just about everything an individual says, sees, or does: the phone calls made, the TV

---

102. ZDnet.com, Facebook and the CIA, by Dennis Howlett, January 14, 2008. https://www.zdnet.com/article/facebook-and-the-cia/.

103. Wikipedia.com, DARPA, https://en.wikipedia.org/wiki/DARPA https://en.wikipedia.org//wiki/DARPA_LifeLog.

shows watched, the magazines read, the plane tickets bought, the email sent and received. Out of this seemingly endless ocean of information, computer scientists would plot distinctive routes in the data, mapping relationships, memories, events, and experiences.

LifeLog's backers said the all-encompassing diary could have turned into a near-perfect digital memory, giving its users computerized assistants with an almost flawless recall of what they had done in the past. But civil libertarians immediately pounced on the project when it debuted last spring (2003), arguing that LifeLog could become the ultimate tool for profiling potential enemies of the state.[104]

You may be saying, "What is wrong with profiling enemies of the state?" But the question I have is, "How do they define *enemies of the state?*"

Could it mean anyone who doesn't agree with all government actions? Could it be a protester exercising his or her First Amendment rights on an issue that is counter to a government action? (Which is the reason it includes "the right to peaceably assemble.")

But the LifeLog project was cancelled, so nothing to worry about anyway, right?

Ironically, Facebook happened to pop up in a dorm room after the LifeLog project was terminated. Facebook coincidentally does pretty much what LifeLog was going to do, except it is now a publicly traded company that makes a lot of money.

If that's not enough coincidence for you, Facebook later hired Regina Dugan, former head of DARPA (the agency that oversaw the LifeLog project) in 2016 to lead their research lab in Menlo Park, California. Although Dugan is no longer with Facebook, I doubt that it is merely coincidental that a woman who was at DARPA's helm, then does a stint with Facebook

104. Wired.com, Pentagon Kills LifeLog Project, February 4, 2004.

and Google. She has since moved on to an autonomous vehicle startup that is working feverishly to get individuals out of their cars.

I am discussing what may seem like useless points of information where social networks and other tech giants are concerned. I bring this up to try to get readers to think about these *coincidences*. I don't believe that the social media and tech giants are harmless cyber czars who continue to have a lot of influence in the role they play, not just on the U.S. stage, but in the entire world.

Facebook, Google, and others collect your data all day long and what are they doing with it? It could be they sell it, make money from it, among a few other things. Why do they need every person's data from cradle to grave?

The latest coincidence is that the government has built a huge data collection center for the U.S. Intelligence Community called the Utah Data Center. It collects and houses everyone's data. Most of the articles I've read on the data collection activities are substantiated in the name of anti-terrorism. I'm not buying it.

An RT.com story published online in 2012 so accurately sums up the reason for data collection in the headline alone, "NSA Utah 'Data Center': Biggest-ever domestic spying lab?" …

> The Utah Data Center will be built on a 240-acre site near Camp Williams, Utah. Once completed in September 2013, it will be twice as large as the US Capitol. The center will provide 100,000 square feet of computer space, out of a total one million square feet. The project, launched in 2010, is to cost the National Security Agency up to $2 billion.
>
> The highly-classified project will be responsible for intercepting, storing and analyzing intelligence data as it zips through both domestic and international networks. The data may come in all

forms: private e-mails, cell phone calls, Google searches—even parking lot tickets or shop purchases.

'This is more than just a data center,' an official source close to the project told the online magazine Wired.com. The source says the center will actually focus on deciphering the accumulated data, essentially code-breaking. This means not only exposing Facebook activities or Wikipedia requests, but compromising "the invisible" Internet, or the "deepnet." Legal and business deals, financial transactions, password-protected files and inter-governmental communications will all become vulnerable. Once communication data is stored, a process known as data-mining will begin. Everything a person does—from traveling to buying groceries—is to be displayed on a graph, allowing the NSA to paint a detailed picture of any given individual's life.[105]

Social media has changed society because now participants are able to personally interact with these communication channels in real-time. When you post data, you are feeding the beast. Every time you post something, be aware that an entity or entities is logging that data and it could be used against you in the future.

In my opinion, this is being done for control—control of every area of your life. Why else would those in control house every piece of data connected to you from your personal communications to purchases, even your Internet search terms. The more data they have on you, the more they know you, and the more they know *how* to control you.

## There's Nothing New Under the Media Sun

I've given readers several examples of the media's deceptive work in my lifetime. I don't think I ever realized how long these people have been

---

105. RT.com, NSA Utah 'Data Center': Biggest-ever domestic spying lab?, March 17, 2012, https://www.rt.com/news/utah-data-center-spy-789/.

intentionally deceiving the masses. I found a great excerpt, a quote from a journalist, very well known in his day, John Swinton. He was Chief Editorial Writer of *The New York Times* during the 1860s. Later he was a freelancer and then Editorial Writer for the *New York Sun* in 1875. He was getting ready to leave the *Sun*, when he gave a speech at a press dinner.

What is astounding to me is as I read this piece of his speech, I found that he used a term to describe the media of his time—it is the same term I used to describe them 140 years later.

Here is a snippet of Swinton's 1883 speech, published in Dr. Richard D. Proctor's book, *Liberty: Will It Survive the 21st Century? Volume 2*:

> "There is no such thing, at this date of the world's history, in America, as an independent press. You know it and I know it....
>
> The business of the journalists is to destroy the truth, to lie outright, to pervert, to vilify, to fawn at the feet of mammon, and to sell his country and his race for his daily bread. You know it and I know it, and what folly is this toasting an independent press? We are the tools and vassals of rich men behind the scenes. We are the jumping jacks they pull the strings and we dance. Our talents, our possibilities, and our lives are all the property of other men. We are intellectual prostitutes."[106]

I believe since it was the end of his career, John Swinton threw caution to the wind, figuring he had nothing to lose at that point. He had already put in his time, had a great career with the Big Media of his day, and probably just wanted to set the record straight. All I know is I would love to have been there that night to see the looks on those journalists' faces. Now that would have been a story!

---

106. Richard D. Proctor, PhD, *Liberty, Will It Survive the 21st Century? Volume 2* (Provis Press, 2016), p. 125.

# CHAPTER 6
# Environment and the Great Reset

In 2000, I first heard about Agenda 21, the United Nations' sustainable development strategy plan, created in 1992, to control people and resources in the name of saving the world from 'global warming' (which has since been renamed climate change). As far back as the 1970s, the press was calling global cooling 'the big environmental threat.'

Global leaders under the United Nations charter were talking about how we had to reduce use of fossil fuels and go back to times when we didn't use the amount of energy that has given us a high standard of living. I remember what stood out in my mind was how they wanted to move people out of the suburbs and back into cities and set aside suburban areas they called "buffer zones" where no humans could go and there would no longer be roads, allowing the lands to grow wild. It seemed so far away at the time, but now twenty some years later, it is on our heels.

Agenda 21 became the 2030 Agenda for Sustainable Development in 2015. I believe this was the major reason the Biden administration has been pushing the Green New Deal—time is running out. It is this plan, built on a foundation of sustainable development, that is connected to the United Nations agenda. Here is how the United Nations defines what they mean by "sustainable development":

## What is sustainable development?

- Sustainable development has been defined as development that meets the needs of the present without compromising the ability of future generations to meet their own needs.

- Sustainable development calls for concerted efforts toward building an inclusive, sustainable, and resilient future for people and the planet.

- For sustainable development to be achieved, it is crucial to harmonize three core elements: economic growth, social inclusion, and environmental protection. These elements are interconnected and all are crucial for the well-being of individuals and societies.

- Eradicating poverty in all its forms and dimensions is an indispensable requirement for sustainable development. To this end, there must be promotion of sustainable, inclusive, and equitable economic growth, creating greater opportunities for all, reducing inequalities, raising basic standards of living, fostering equitable social development and inclusion, and promoting integrated and sustainable management of natural resources and ecosystems.[107]

This sounds warm and fuzzy, but when you look into their agenda goals, you detect the strategy being used to raise standards of living in some countries, means reducing and dragging down the standards in other developed countries, bringing all to third world standards—that is the only way to make everything equal.

Also, who defines "meeting the needs of the present without compromising the ability of future generations" and what does this mean? What does building a sustainable future mean? Who gets to judge what changes in lifestyles and societies will be made to reach these goals? It does not

---

107. www.un.org, The Sustainable Development Agenda, FAQs,
https://www.un.org/sustainabledevelopment/development-agenda.

appear that the average citizen gets a say in how this will be conducted. It appears that it will be an edict sent to the rest of us by those who hold high positions within the United Nations organization of unelected members.

The last point about eradicating poverty seems like a very noble goal; who wouldn't want to get rid of world poverty? But who gets to select which natural resources to use or to scrap? What equitable social development and inclusion or exclusion are the promoters referring to? Will they decide to exclude from society those who don't agree with their decisions?

Note the major pillars they touch on: "economic growth, social inclusion, and environmental protection." I suspect they likely want control of these areas in order to keep a leash on the people who don't agree with their agenda.

In my opinion, *environment protection*, will be the overall linchpin on which everything else will hinge. Their overall philosophy is that humans should be secondary to the environment and climate since, in their opinion, we have been ruining the planet. This is the urgency they used in the United States to try to push through the Green New Deal in 2019, introduced as a congressional resolution by Democrats.

This plan has many agendas, but the bottom line is that the UN agenda goal is to use the plan for wealth redistribution worldwide; to make everyone equal economically; to have access to limited resources, using almost no energy, limiting travel and mobility geographically; taking away private property rights; population reduction, and—once again—to control all people and everything all of the time. This is the recurring theme across the pillars of society that I discuss throughout this book.

Someone who knows firsthand about this agenda to rewild and confiscate private lands from Americans, including farmers and ranchers, is Debbie Bacigalupi, a writer, editor, speaker, and activist. In 2016, I interviewed her as she was helping fight for her parents' land rights.

Here is an excerpt from our interview regarding her story:

> My parents have a beautiful, beautiful ranch that they've
> worked their entire adult life to earn enough money to buy
> their dream and to continue my father's side of the family legacy
> of being California generational cattle ranchers and farmers.
> And so we've got a river running through our property. We have
> diversions, we have ditches that feed our grass, water our grass,
> that then water our grass-fed cows. And my dad, who's a con-
> struction engineer, a professional civil engineer, put in ponds
> for conservation. And we love wildlife. We love seeing animals
> on our property.
>
> … the California Department of Fish and Game, which is what
> it was called back then, it's now Fish and Wildlife because the
> 21st century is not about game, it's about rewilding America
> … what happened is my parents, who have historically been
> friends with Fish and Game and the wardens—I mean, the
> wardens used to come to our ranch and have coffee with my
> parents and just talk about what was going on, and all of a
> sudden, they showed up in bulletproof jackets and flanked my
> parents. They were armed and flanked my parents on either side
> and were saying, "Why aren't you signing on to this thing called
> the Incidental Take Permit?
>
> And what the ITP is, is any time an endangered fish, like a
> salmon, for example, is found on your property dead, it could
> be as much as a $25,000 fine per fish. But at the same time,
> signing on to this Incidental Take Permit, you put your money
> into a bucket. And if a fish, a dead fish, is found on your prop-
> erty, that bucket of collected money from all the ranchers and
> farmers who sign on to this thing, you could use that money
> to help offset or mitigate the dead fish that is found on your
> property. It gives Fish and Game or the government the right to

trespass on your property. And my dad and mom were like, this is illegal. It's not Constitutional. We're not signing on to it. But they started getting pressure from California state agencies to sign on.[108]

Bacigalupi started attending conferences on sustainable development, including some connected to the United Nations. This is when she started learning about the agenda to take power from Americans, specifically, their private property rights.

She explained how Agenda 21, created in 1992, was an offshoot of the United Nations Rio Earth Summit. On a national level, the Clinton administration put forth an Executive Order 12852 that established the President's Council on Sustainable Development in 1993; the Clinton and Bush administrations and every one since from both the Republican and Democrat parties have been supporting some of the UN agenda goals—including buffer zones that are lands they plan to take away from the private sector to supposedly protect them.

According to a document from Bill Clinton's President's Council on Sustainable Development Task Force, "Agenda 21 will require a profound reorientation of all human society unlike anything the world has ever experienced. A major shift in the priorities of both governments and individuals ... an unprecedented redeployment of human and financial resources... ."[109]

In our interview, Bacigalupi continues reading the document and expands her ideas on the subject ...

This shift will demand that a concern for the environmental consequences of every human action, it says it right here. Every-

---

108. *The Truth Seekers Radio Show*: Episode 59; Interview with Debbie Bacigalupi, "Private property rights and the United Nations," 2016.

109. The Road to Sustainable Development: A Snapshot of Activities in the United States, https://clinton-whitehouse3.archives.gov/PCSD/Publications/Snapshot.html the Clinton Administration, March 1997.

human-action - we are breathing right now, that is a human action. We are alive, we are awake, we are blinking. Every human action will be integrated into individual and collective decision making at every level. Why? Because they claim that every human action has an environmental consequence so therefore, according to this whole movement … they have this idea that if they can scare us into believing that we human beings and that our human actions are causing this catastrophic devastation to the Earth, like global warming … it will scare us into changing our behavior… .[110]

In my opinion, the international group of elitists has been using the "saving the environment" card as a tool to capture adherence to their agenda plan on a global scale. You see, if you scare everyone around the world by saying that the environment of the planet we share is at great peril, then you have license to regulate every area of life for everyone around the world in the name of saving the planet. And who would not want to save the planet? What they don't tell you is how your life will change drastically to third-world conditions.

The elitist group of people implementing these rules won't change their behaviors or lifestyle. They believe they should be exempt; they just don't tell you that.

Maurice Strong, Secretary General of the UN Conference on Environment and Development, expressed his belief at the UN Earth Climate Summit in 1992 that it is the fault of the middle class, not the elite class flying around in jets on a whim, that is responsible for climate change. "It is clear that current lifestyles and consumption patterns of the affluent middle class … involving high meat intake, consumption of large amounts of frozen and convenience foods, ownership of motor vehicles,

---

110. *The Truth Seekers Radio Show*: Episode 59; Interview with Debbie Bacigalupi, "Private property rights and the United Nations," 2016.

golf courses, small electric appliances, home and work place air-conditioning, and suburban housing are not sustainable.... . A shift is necessary toward lifestyles less geared to environmentally damaging consumption patterns." [111]

As the elite class want us to stay put and limit travel, move to electric vehicles that have limitations on mileage, eat manufactured fake meat products and other genetically modified foods, and go without air-conditioning or heating in our homes, these elitists will continue to jet around the world, eat the finest foods, drink the finest wines, and will not change their lifestyle, but will completely tear down our standard of living to third-world levels—oh yes, and by the way, we will be paying for these changes through global taxes they plan to put on our backs.

## Trust the Science, Whose Science?

I for one am tired of hearing how we have to believe their science. Of course you can manufacture any scientific outcome when you have the money to conduct studies, buy the outcomes that fit your agendas, prop up your bought-and-paid-for scientists to parrot those outcomes as "real science," muzzle the scientists who don't agree with your outcomes, and put out press releases for the mainstream lapdog press to grab onto and disseminate lies.

There is an interesting communications model outlined by German political scientist Elisabeth Noelle-Neumann, in a work called, *The Spiral of Science: Public Opinion-Our Social Skin*. The following is an explanation based on Noelle-Neumann's work from Shelia Zilinsky, author of *Green Gospel: The New World Religion*. She explains how those in power use a strategy to silence those in academia, or anyone opposed to any main-

---

111. Forbes.com, The U.N.'s Global Warming War On Capitalism: An Important History Lesson, Larry Bell, Jan. 2013. https://www.forbes.com/sites/larrybell/2013/01/22/ the-u-n-s-global-warming-war-on-capitalism-an-important-history-lesson-2/?sh=5a1ca829be69.

stream narrative of choice, from speaking out against it.

"People with strong ethics are always at a disadvantage when debating people who have no ethics. This is because the public doesn't have the experience to know who is telling the truth ... the key is perception, not reality. They only have to convince the public that a majority of "scientists" believes a certain way, even if that is untrue. If they are successful creating this perception the others usually remain silent ... that's because power resides with majority opinion, not the truth."[112]

Zilinsky gives an example of how the United Nation's climate facade is easily carried out. In 1998, the United Nations created a scientific and intergovernmental body called The Intergovernmental Panel on Climate Change (IPCC). It is their job to create reports that support the UN's climate change narrative. According to Zilinsky, they do not do research or any monitoring of their own. From what I could tell by the reports they publish on their website, it is made up of a group of writers and editors (270 authors from 67 countries) that have supposedly assessed the impacts of climate change around the world. They are nominated and selected to write and publish these reports. So if a writer subscribes to their narrative, they could be a part of this group. Zilinksy writes:

> Most think the IPCC is the authority on global warming and climate change ... their role was to provide scientific proof that human production of CO2 resulted in runaway global warming. They manipulated data and created false methods, while ignoring standard scientific procedures. They fooled most scientists, who simply accepted the claims at face value, not imagining there were scientists who would do such things.
>
> German meteorologist and physicist Klaus-Eckert Puls explains, 'Ten years ago, I simply parroted what the IPCC told us. One

---

112. Sheila Zilinsky, *Green Gospel: The New World Religion* (Redemption Press, 2015), p 81-82.

day I started checking the facts and data. At first, I started with a sense of doubt, but then I became outraged when I discovered that what the IPCC and the media were telling us was sheer nonsense and was not even supported by any scientific facts and measurements. To this day I feel shame that as a scientist I made presentations of their science without first checking it... Scientifically it is a sheer absurdity to think we can get a nice climate by turning a CO2 adjustment knob.'[113]

While doing more research on Klaus-Eckert Puls, I stumbled onto an organization website called The European Institute for Climate and Energy, a private German think tank founded in 2007 and funded by voluntary contributions, " ... an association of a growing number of nature, humanities and economists, engineers, journalists and politicians who regard the assertion of climate change as solely 'man-made' as not scientifically rigorous and neglects known solar and other natural influences."[114]

Here are some assertions from The European Institute for Climate and Energy in regard to climate change. These assertions go against the mainstream establishment narrative:

**Climate Zones:** "There is no 'global climate,' only climate zones from polar to tropical. The climate of all climate zones on earth has never been constant. Climate changes are the rule. There have been rapid and slow climate changes, with trends often even opposing in different regions, and they still are today... ."[115]

> **Climate Before vs. Climate Now:** The recent climate change, which is due to natural causes, is comparatively moderate. It is now generally scientifically recognized that in earlier geo-

---

113. Ibid., 82-83.

114. EIKE (European Institute for Climate and Energy) https://eike-klima-energie.eu/about-us/.

115. EIKE (European Institute for Climate and Energy), Climate Policy Paper. https://eike-klima-energie.eu/die-mission/grundsatzpapier-klima/.

logical periods there were incomparably more violent climatic changes... .Favorable for the people and associated with a significant increase in population as a result of better harvests was e.g. B. the Medieval Warm Period (ca. 1000 to 1300).

On the other hand, the "Little Ice Age" (approx. 1400-1800) had a catastrophic effect, the coldest phase of which occurred in the second half of the seventeenth century together with the solar Maunder minimum.

While today we are talking about temperature changes of a few tenths of a degree over the last hundred years, the people of the Vistula glacial period (approx. 120,000-10,000 BC) experienced climatic jumps of several degrees during their lifetimes.

Glaciologists note that temperatures have been warmer two-thirds of the time over the past 10,000 years than they are today. Therefore, the Alpine glaciers had almost disappeared in all strong warm periods, for example, when Hannibal crossed the Alps with elephants. In the hot summers of the medieval warm period, European rivers hardly carried any water. The foundations of the famous Regensburg stone bridge could be built in the dry Danube and the people of Cologne could cross the Rhine with dry feet.[116]

**CO2:** "CO2 is the basic component of photosynthesis and therefore a prerequisite for all life on earth. Plants grow better with increasing CO2 concentration: The grain yields in the field increase. Greenhouse cultures are gassed with CO2 to increase yield."[117]

**Politics and Climate:** "To date, no significant or even uniform warming trend has been found for the southern hemisphere. Antarctica continues to cool. The recent warming of the northern hemisphere in the 20th

---

116. EIKE (European Institute for Climate and Energy), Climate Policy Paper. https://eike-klima-energie.eu/die-mission/grundsatzpapier-klima/.

117. Ibid.

century, which is minor compared to climate history, prompted the UN to found the IPCC [Intergovernmental Panel on Climate

Change] … the aim was and is to provide the national governments with the propagandistic basis for drastic changes in their energy and fiscal policies… ."[118]

And there it is, "drastic changes in their energy and fiscal policies… ." I believe the entire climate change narrative is about taking control through food, energy, and money. $CO_2$ is the new boogie man they need to do this. How would you get rid of all $CO_2$? Remove all living things? Would that be enough for these people?

If you are a person of faith, and you believe their science when you know an agenda is attached, how can you *not* look into the issues I have presented here?

If you believe we were created by a Creator, do you believe that a Creator would have created humans to expel $CO_2$ that would then destroy the very environment that was created for them? The same can be said for animals and plants—the natural order of life is to uptake oxygen and release carbon dioxide. Would it make sense that emitting $CO_2$ back into their environment would be deadly to it? This does not make sense; yet this is what they claim.

## Explaining the Changes

So if there is no real climate change, how do you explain the recent floods, wildfires, droughts, drastic temperature changes, erratic, non-characteristic weather in different regions, etc.? I have never said these things do not exist. My argument is that it is not the average low or middle class citizen who is causing most of this activity. I contend it is the upper echelon that I have been mentioning throughout the chapters of this book—

118. Ibid.

the people with the money and control (through military, government, and technological means).

So the next obvious question would be, "What is the source of these non-characteristic and erratic events?"

I have studied this topic for years. Originally I found that the United States has had weather modification capability since World War II. I cannot verify this, but I have seen United States documentation going back to the 1960s and 1970s.

If this is true, can you imagine the technological capabilities governments have today that may not be common knowledge?

## History of Weather Modification and Research

Dane Wigington, researcher, speaker, author, filmmaker, and radio host, has studied what he calls, "geoengineering" for more than twenty years. Geoengineering means the climate is being manipulated through technological means, causing environmental changes and destruction, and even health dangers.

Wigington's work explains how this first came to his attention; skies that were normally blue and clear were now mostly milky and muted. I identified with this because I grew up in South Florida, and I remember when we had blue, vibrant skies most of the time. By the mid-1990s, daily white streaks in the sky would expand until you could barely see blue sky and the sunshine was muted. If you grew up in a colder, less tropical area of the country, it probably was not as noticeable, but in South Florida it was obvious.

The ability to manipulate the weather was documented in a U.S. government report published in November 1966 called: "A Recommended National Program in Weather Modification," a report to the Interdepartmental Committee for Atmospheric Sciences (ICAS).

An attached memorandum, with the subject line Weather Modification Program, stated that there was some concern as to what was being done in weather modification and by whom, " ... the Federal Council asked ICAS to prepare a report outlining 'who is doing what in weather modification, the future plans of the agencies (particularly Commerce and Interior) and their interrelationships, and the considerations that should affect decisions on the division of responsibilities for research in weather modification.'"[119]

The report introduction says it all, and it seems there was real concern as to what could be done in weather modification more than fifty years ago. Could they have suspected what Wigington is finding today in his research? The report introduction continues:

> The earth's weather has a profound influence on agriculture, forestry, water resources, industry, commerce, transportation, construction, field operations, commercial fishing, and many other human activities. Adverse effects of weather on man's activities and the earth's resources are extremely costly, amounting to billions of dollars per year, sometimes causing irreparable damage as when human lives are lost in severe storms.
>
> There is, therefore, great motivation to develop effective countermeasures against the destructive effects of weather, and, conversely, to enhance the beneficial aspects. The financial and other benefits to human welfare of being able to modify weather to augment water supplies, reduce lightning, suppress hail, mitigate tornadoes, and inhibit the full development of hurricanes would be very great.[120]

Notice the author says, "to enhance the beneficial aspects." What are

---

119. Geo Engineering Watch, documents: A Recommended National Program in Weather Modification; a Report to the Interdepartmental Committee for Atmospheric Sciences, by Homer E. Newell, https://www.geoengineeringwatch.org/documents/19680002906_1968002906.pdf, Nov. 1966, p. 3.
120. Ibid., p. 5.

the beneficial aspects? Could those beneficial aspects vary based on whom you ask, or who happens to be in control at the time? It is my belief that some of these beneficial aspects have been changed throughout the decades. As the players have changed, I am sure the agendas and goals have changed over time. Could they have become more sinister? Do you think those in charge who have something to gain might lose focus on what *is really* in the best interest of the average person in our country and around the world?

There was weather modification dating as far back as the 1940s. Here is a quote from the report that would corroborate the assertion that experimentation dated back to that time.

> Over the past twenty years experiments have been conducted on weather modification, particularly on the effects of *seeding* clouds with such materials as silver iodide crystals. The results are limited. Under suitable circumstances it has been possible to augment precipitation by ten to twenty percent, and to reduce the frequency of fire-producing lightning strikes. Effects on hail production have been noted, sometimes suppression and sometimes augmentation … The limited success to date is encouraging, and underscores the importance of pressing forward with the necessary research to understand the dynamics of weather systems that will have to be dealt with in any efforts at weather modification."[121]

The report goes on to outline specific recommendations that should be the major focus: budgets, weather modification in agriculture, water resources, augmenting precipitation in areas of the country, seeding clouds with pyrotechnics, hail suppression, and much more. It also mentions

---

121. Geo Engineering Watch, documents: A Recommended National Program in Weather Modification; a Report to the Interdepartmental Committee for Atmospheric Sciences, by Homer E. Newell, https://www.geoengineeringwatch.org/documents/19680002906_1968002906.pdf, Nov. 1966, p. 5-6.

areas throughout the country from east to west.

A couple of interesting side notes also mentioned in the report were a Federal Aviation Agency Weather Modification Program and a NASA Panel to Study Weather Modification Activities. It seems glaringly possible that if the FAA and NASA were weighing in on weather modification in the early 1960s, something must have prompted their response on the subject.

## Climate Modification and CO2

I found another interesting document on Wigington's research website from weather modification hearings that took place in January and March of 1974. It was titled, "Hearings before the Subcommittee on Oceans and International Environment of the Committee on Foreign Relations United States Senate." The subtitle made a note of "the need for an international agreement prohibiting the use of environmental and geophysical modification as weapons of war."[122]

While I was focused on the international aspect of this hearing, I found other golden nuggets in this document amazing. Senator Claiborne Pell (D) of Rhode Island asked Professor Gordon J. F. MacDonald, Associate Director of the Institute of Geophysics and Planetary Physics at the University of California, Los Angeles, if he could insert a copy of an article Professor MacDonald wrote in 1966 titled, "How to Wreck the Environment."

This article was a buffet of all of the experiments and research that had been conducted. Some of the topics it covered were: weather modification, climate modification, future weather and climate modification, earthquake modification, ocean modification, and brain waves.

---

122. Geo Engineering Watch, documents: Weather Modification; Hearings before the Subcommittee on Oceans and International Environment of the Committee on Foreign Relations United States Senate, https://www.geoengineeringwatch.org/documents/GeoengineeringWatch%20-%20Weather%20Modification%20Hearings%201974.pdf, March 1974, p. 1.

I found interesting information in the climate modification section very telling because the things the professor said in 1966 *totally negate the climate change mantra of today.*

In his opening, Professor MacDonald revealed the technological climate modification capabilities they already had at the time he wrote the article. He cautions that these technologies could be used as weapons and could potentially cause great damage.

"Among future means of obtaining national objectives by force, one possibility hinges on man's ability to control and manipulate the environment of his planet. When achieved, this power over his environment will provide man with a new force capable of doing great and indiscriminate damage … as I will argue, these weapons are peculiarly suited for covert or secret wars."[123]

He was basically saying that those who control the weather and have power over the environment can obtain their objectives by force from an unsuspecting victim. He said *national objectives,* which I would substitute with *international objectives.* He ends the statement saying these weapons are suited for secret wars.

If the people of this world are being sold a lie about the climate and environment, and manipulation can change their way of life and break them down financially, I would call that a secret war. I don't know that the professor was thinking about the United Nations climate trick when he wrote this, but I am saying he is telling us at the very least that weather manipulation is possible.

The good professor also describes differences in climate change over the course of history; if I did not know better, I would say other periods in history had a climate emergency too, but somehow nature seemed to take care of it—all without edicts from the United Nations—imagine that!

---

123. Ibid., p. 56.

It is important to emphasize some points from Professor MacDonald's article in 1966 and put them in the context of today's climate change mantra:

"It is useful to examine climate variations under natural conditions. Firm geological evidence exists of a long sequence of Ice Ages, in the relatively recent past, which shows that the world's climate has been in a state of slow evolution. There is also good geological, archeological, and historical evidence for a pattern of smaller, more rapid fluctuations superimposed on the slow evolutionary change. For example, in Europe the climate of the early period following the last Ice Age was continental, with hot summers and cold winters."[124]

Notice the professor says that under *natural conditions* without modification, there is still evidence of long periods of ice ages and this is in the recent past. So he is admitting that these extreme temperature periods are part of our environment's "natural conditions"—removing the ice age periods from a phenomenon created by people and their lifestyles. He also points out there are slow, natural changes he calls a slow evolution and patterns of smaller, quicker changes. This may mean that some regions may experience more drastic changes than other regions. This does not mean all areas are chaotic all the time. The evolution he is talking about in the natural conditions may also be part of nature's way of renewal, taking place in different regions at different times. The professor's article expands on these ideas:

> In the sixth millennium BC, there was a change to a warm humid climate with a mean temperature of five degrees Fahrenheit higher than at present and a heavy rainfall that caused considerable growth of peat. This period, known as a

---

124. Geo Engineering Watch, documents: Weather Modification; Hearings before the Subcommittee on Oceans and International Environment of the Committee on Foreign Relations United States Senate, https://www.geoengineeringwatch.org/documents/GeoengineeringWatch%20-%20Weather%20Modification%20Hearings%201974.pdf. March 1974, p. 58.

climatic optimum, was accentuated in Scandinavia by a land subsidence that permitted a greater influx of warm Atlantic water into the large Baltic Sea.

The climatic optimum was peculiar. While on the whole there was a very gradual decrease of rainfall, the decrease was interrupted by long droughts during which the surface peat dried. This fluctuation occurred several times, the main dry periods being from 2000 to 1900, 1200 to 1000, and 700 to 500 BC. The last, a dry heat wave lasting approximately 200 years, was the best developed. The drought, though not sufficiently intense to interrupt the steady development of forests, did cause extensive migrations of peoples from drier to wetter regions.[125]

MacDonald states above that in an earlier time, the temperature was warmer than at the time the article was written by "five degrees Fahrenheit higher," and yet those temperatures changed again throughout history. Does this mean the people of the sixth millennium BC were emitting too much CO2, or was it due to natural conditions of the time? His article also documents dry periods in history that brought about drought conditions so severe they caused people to move to different regions; yet, conditions evened out again to a new equilibrium until the next change in conditions.

His historical accounts of weather patterns for periods seem to change and then change again. It also seems like the variations are across the board geographically. So how did this become an emergency of late? I don't think you will find this account in any United Nations literature.

Professor MacDonald's 1966 article also mentions CO2, the climate change movement's biggest enemy.

"Carbon dioxide placed in the atmosphere since the start of the industrial revolution has produced an increase in the average temperature of the

125. Ibid.

lower atmosphere of a few tenths of a degree Fahrenheit."[126]

U.S. industrialization started in the late 1700s, but the American Industrial Revolution started in the 1870s. Almost 100 years later, Professor MacDonald writes this article and says the average temperature increased by a *few tenths of a degree Fahrenheit*. Should a few tenths of a degree every one hundred years cause the concern and urgency that the United Nations agenda is pushing? Also, take into account the technological improvements and current EPA regulations and restrictions that have been implemented in the United States. They were put into place to curb the environmental damage they say is happening.

The professor also mentions $CO_2$ experiments. He does not say they are ridding the earth of $CO_2$—but to the contrary—spreading it through cloud seeding with silver iodide.

"Experiments over the past eighteen years have demonstrated unequivocally that clouds composed of supercooled water droplets can be transformed into ice-crystal clouds by seeding them with silver iodide, "dry ice" (frozen carbon dioxide), and other suitable chemical agents. This discovery has been applied operationally in the clearance of airports covered by supercooled ground fog."[127]

Did he say, "carbon dioxide"? Are these the same $CO_2$ emissions they rail against? So are they seeding clouds with $CO_2$ and then blaming it on people and their activities and animal digestive gases being released into the atmosphere? Could they be creating the problem so that they can also have the solution and ultimately worldwide control?

MacDonald also mentions the military having the ability to disperse material into the upper atmosphere to help either cool or warm the sur-

126. Geo Engineering Watch, documents: Weather Modification; Hearings before the Subcommittee on Oceans and International Environment of the Committee on Foreign Relations United States Senate, https://www.geoengineeringwatch.org/documents/GeoengineeringWatch%20-%20Weather%20Modification%20Hearings%201974.pdf. March 1974, p. 59.

127. Ibid., p. 57.

face. Does this mean they could have been doing this in recent decades to help build a public perception of drastic warming or cooling, erratic changes to the climate, to move nations into their control agenda?

I believe that among the pillars of society, the environment is the linchpin they are using to move nations to a global government. One reason is that climate issues have international reach. It is not just a United States problem, or a Mexico problem, or whatever country you name. It is an issue that reaches all countries, ethnicities, languages, religions, peoples, etc. Ironically, Professor MacDonald ends his article making the point that in spite of both environmental issues and deliberate climate modification technologies, they will still have to overcome traditional institutional concepts.

> The environment knows no political boundaries; it is independent of the institutions based on geography, and the effects of modification can be projected from any one point to any other on the earth … environmental modification may be a dominant feature of future world decades, there is concern that this incipient technology is in total conflict with many of the traditional geographical and political units and concepts … political, legal, economic, and sociological consequences of deliberate environmental modification, even for peaceful purposes, will be of such complexity that perhaps all our present involvements in nuclear affairs will seem simple.[128]

I've shown that at the very least, it is possible that our government has had the power to manipulate our weather and the environment as far back as the 1940s. Notice I said "manipulate." I still contend they are deliberately manipulating the climate to scare people around the world, to cull the masses, to get them in line and to sign onto the global agenda.

---

128. Ibid., p. 64.

If they were using pyrotechnics in cloud manipulation back in the late 1960s, what could they *not* do today?

## The Great Reset: How Will Your Life Change?

Whether or not you believe that they may be intentionally modifying the weather, they are moving forward with an agenda to "reset" our way of life—and as I stated earlier, it is based on climate change—or as I believe, climate manipulation.

In June 2022, the World Economic Forum (WEF) announced what they call, The Great Reset. Those playing a key role in the rollout include the United Nations, World Economic Forum, International Monetary Fund, British monarchy, and the Chinese Communist Party. I believe that these are just the public faces; I believe a group of elite behind them are driving the reset.

Those are the "who," but just "what" is the Great Reset agenda about? Journalist, author, and radio host Alex Newman sums it up succinctly in his article, "Great Reset: Happening Now."

"The Great Reset agenda involves a fundamental transformation of absolutely everything. It is a scheme so massive, so draconian, and so ubiquitous that even books could not cover it all. Its advocates are openly saying as much, with WEF head Klaus Schwab declaring that 'all aspects of our societies and economies' need to be 'revamped,' including the 'social contract.' An infamous 2016 WEF video offering "predictions" of coming neo-feudalism claimed that by 2030, people would "own nothing." Even "our thinking and behavior" will have to dramatically shift, Schwab declared in announcing the Great Reset."[129]

As I've stated earlier, this cast of characters is working on an agenda

---

129. TheNewAmerican.com, Great Reset: Happening Now, by Alex Newman, November 14, 2022, https://thenewamerican.com/great-reset-happening-now/.

that at its foundation is about controlling all areas of our lives; controlling all systems of our societies globally. They want control in environment, business, education, government, media, technology, religion, science, healthcare, economy, banking, even social media.

One of the strategies to reach their goals is to move everything to digital platforms. This will be the base of their control capabilities that include surveillance of everything and everyone. If you've never heard about this, I must admit it sounds insane, like a science fiction story; unfortunately, it is not a story—it is true.

But "how" will they do this? Do you wonder why there is so much chaos in our world now? Some of it is organic, but I think most of it has been planned for a long time and is now being carried out to move us swiftly into this new system. I think this is part of the Agenda 2030. It is not only about the environment, but it is about the money system too.

Newman answers the "how" they do this in his article, and it is based on what is called an "ESG" model of investing—Environmental, Social, Corporate Governance, "which is simply the latest marketing slogan to promote a much older idea: a fascistic economic model. Under the ESG model, corporations are expected to serve the goals and decrees of the state and the predatory elites, rather than consumers and shareholders as they have done historically in the free market."[130]

These statements support what we see taking place in society today with mega corporations. They seem to be committing financial suicide as they ignore the values and needs of their customers and instead entertain and push a "woke culture"—even if it means losing those customers.

According to Newman, the ESG term was created by Paul Clements-Hunt, a United Nations globalist who served as head of their Environment Programme (UNEP) Finance Initiative.

---

130. Ibid.

The "ESG" model is strictly tied not only to globalism, but also to very left-wing progressive politics, so if you do not believe this way, you may be in for trouble, especially if you speak against it.

To demonstrate how this model would work as a strategy to coerce the public into obedience, I share this exchange from when I interviewed Executive Director of Citizens for Free Speech, speaker, and author of *Technocracy Rising: The Trojan Horse of Global Transformation,* Patrick Wood, about a similar term you may have heard of called the 'social credit score.' This is a similar ideology. In my opinion, it imposes strict penalties against people when they speak out about something or don't want to go along with something that may be against their morals and values.

In 2016, Wood spoke about a strategy to social engineer peoples' thoughts and behaviors, and he said that it was already underway in China. According to Wood:

> Here's what they're doing in China right now. The social score is not actually just credit. When we say credit score, you think of when you go to apply for a loan, and if you have a 750 credit score where you just get automatic approval or whatever.
>
> But what they're doing in China is that the government is shifting all the social media plus all the financial records ... And they're using a complex artificial intelligence program to assign a value to every citizen depending on how loyal and how compatible they are with the government. And it's scary in the sense that you don't have any way to track any data. If you end up with a score that's in the tank, you don't have any way to correct that data if it's wrong.
>
> The scores are being calculated, and they're publishing those scores on social media. So let's say you have a hundred friends on the equivalent of Facebook in China and all these other friends, let's say, have a relatively high score or social score, say

800. And let's say that your score is lower because you're a little bit of a rabble rouser and a troublemaker, and you're criticizing the government policies on this, that, or the other; let's say your score is only 400. Well, they publish your score so that all your good little government friends know that you don't fit. And so they begin to put social pressure on you to comply, and you will find yourself shunned because part of the calculation of the social score is how many friends you have on social media who are troublemakers.[131]

So Wood is saying that if you don't toe a certain political, social, or even religious line, you could be in for trouble. This social score is one small part of the entire puzzle. There are many other prongs to this new global system, but if for some reason you are out of the system because of your morals, beliefs, or speech, you could be locked out of *their* system—no access to banking, money, education, services, or even a job.

I believe governments need big corporations to help carry out their scheme. I have noticed for the last few years, how it seems many big corporations that used to remain apolitical are publicly taking the leftist, progressive stance, even if it means losing right-wing or conservative customers. It no longer seems to matter to them.

This is what I call real *fascism*, or *corporate fascism*. It's an ideology based on a relationship between business and the centralized government; in other words, big business and government work together to take control of the marketplace, and ultimately, the people. Some companies and firms that Newman names in his article have adopted this global fascist agenda including Visa, Bank of America, Johnson & Johnson, MasterCard, Salesforce, the Ford Foundation, the Rockefeller Foundation, and more.

To answer the questions, "Where will this happen?" and "When will

---

131. Truth Seekers Radio Show; Episode 60, Patrick Wood, author of *Technocracy Rising: The Trojan Horse of Global Transformation*, 2016.

this happen?" the "Where?" is *everywhere*! The "when" is *now*!

Banking and money are other aspects they need to reset for this system to become implemented worldwide. Especially if they want to control our movement, where and what we buy, where and how we work, where we live, what we eat, and they don't want us to own anything. Enter the Central Bank Digital Currency, the CBDC, that I mentioned in Chapter 3. This is the digital currency the Federal Reserve is planning to release. They have to do away with cash and implement a digital currency that only they will control.

Here is a statement from Newman's research about the coming cashless society:

> As cash is increasingly demonized and sidelined, governments and central banks are already working to replace it with the Central Bank Digital Currencies.... In early October, the Bank for International Settlements (BIS)—a sort of central bank for the central banks of the world—announced that it had successfully completed its CBDC pilot program to promote multi-currency cross-border payments. This came after the BIS 'Innovation Hub,' which created 'strategic partnerships' with the Federal Reserve and other central banks, guided monetary authorities around the world in the development of the ideas and technology.... With cash out of the way and everyone dependent on 'digital' currencies to buy and sell in the marketplace, and with proposals to make it 'programmable,' the potential for tyranny is unlimited.[132]

I know this is unbelievable and antithetical to our current way of life including free speech; ability to worship how you wish (or not); live where you want; travel where you want, or shop where you want. These freedoms

---

132. TheNewAmerican.com, Great Reset: Happening Now, by Alex Newman, November 14, 2022. https://thenewamerican.com/great-reset-happening-now/.

we have enjoyed will be, as Klaus Schwab stated, "revamped." *If you think I am crazy and this all sounds outlandish, I don't blame you.* All I ask is that you try to prove me wrong; somehow, I believe you will find the truth.

CHAPTER 7
# The Pandemic Chronicles

W hen I started writing this book, China was going through the beginning stages of the Covid pandemic. In 2023, I saw a news headline that said the World Health Organization has announced the end of the Covid global health emergency. [133]

Of course, I thought about addressing the virus earlier, but my head was still swirling from the tentacles that extend from the virus. At the time, I tried to stay away from news reports, both mainstream and independent, just to keep my sanity. If all you watched was Covid coverage 24/7, it would kill your spirit because of the constant negativity. Still every once in a while, I'd catch a headline here or there—and even that was discouraging, so I stopped.

So how did I get to this place? During the pandemic, I was checking my email messages one morning and an email headline led me down a rabbit hole of no return and before I knew it, I was on a website at the Johns Hopkins Center for Health Security.

Let me say that again—this was *not* a conservative news site or blog.

---

133. CNN.com, WHO says Covid-19 is no longer a global health emergency, May 5, 2023, https://www.cnn.com/2023/05/05/health/who-ends-covid-health-emergency/index.html.

It was as elite and mainstream as you can get, Johns Hopkins, a prestigious and world-renowned source in healthcare. Everything I am going to describe next is on this website (at least today) and available to the public, for all to read.

## Event 201 – The Dress Rehearsal

A page on this Johns Hopkins site describes a mock pandemic exercise that took place October 18, 2019, called Event 201. Following is the introductory sentence for the event hosted by the Johns Hopkins Center for Health Security.

The title was, "Statement about nCoV (*novel coronavirus*)and our pandemic exercise."

Did you catch that phrase—"our pandemic exercise"? This is referring to the mock pandemic that took place in New York in the fall of 2019. The website's introduction continues, "In October 2019, the Johns Hopkins Center for Health Security hosted a pandemic tabletop exercise called "Event 201" with partners, the World Economic Forum (WEF), and the Bill and Melinda Gates Foundation."[134]

This is telling us that Johns Hopkins, the World Economic Forum, and the Bill and Melinda Gates Foundation hosted a mock pandemic exercise called Event 201, just one month before China, and then the world started to experience this pandemic in real time. Was the timing of this event a mere coincidence?

Before I move on, I want to make quick mention of something. You've probably heard of the World Economic Forum at one time or another, but what are they about? What do they do?

In case you are not sure, here is a quote from their website: "The World

---

134. Centerforhealthsecurity.org, Johns Hopkins Bloomberg School of Public Health, Statement about nCoV and our pandemic exercise (Johns Hopkins, orig. published Jan. 2020), https://centerforhealthsecurity.org/2020/statement-about-ncov-and-our-pandemic-exercise-0.

Economic Forum is the International Organization for Public-Private Cooperation. The Forum engages the foremost political, business, cultural and other leaders of society to shape global, regional, and industry agendas."[135]

It goes on to say it was established in 1971 as a not-for-profit foundation headquartered in Geneva, Switzerland. But let's revisit what they said in their quote, "The Forum engages the foremost political, business, cultural, and other leaders of society to shape global, regional and industry agendas."[136]

So they work with politicians, big business, cultural influencers (Hollywood movers and shakers, the entertainment industry, news organizations, social media kingpins) to push out their agendas. I said "big business" because I doubt they are working with mom and pop businesses to get *their* input on what's best. Most likely they are working with big corporations like Pfizer, Ford Motor Company, Walmart, and the like.

The point I want to make about the World Economic Forum is they have their tentacles in all types of institutions throughout the world to, in my opinion, help push out their agendas. Again, the agendas they claimed on their website were, "to shape global, regional, and industry agendas."

Now back to the Johns Hopkins statement about the dry run for the Covid pandemic called Event 201. The following quote is from a web page created specifically for Event 201, and it describes the reason for the pandemic exercise.

"The Johns Hopkins Center for Health Security in partnership with the World Economic Forum and the Bill and Melinda Gates Foundation hosted Event 201, a high-level pandemic exercise on October 18, 2019, in New York, NY. The exercise illustrated areas where public/private partner-

---

135. Weforum.org, The World Economic Forum, Our Mission, https://www.weforum.org/about/world-economic-forum.

136. Ibid.

ships will be necessary during the response to a severe pandemic in order to diminish large-scale economic and societal consequences."[137]

Did you notice the phrase, "public, private partnerships"? This was the language in the mission of the World Economic Forum I stated earlier. Translated, it means that agendas, narratives, and actions are determined by elites at the top to be pushed downstream to get full cooperation from governments (local, state, regional), big business, healthcare establishments, educational institutions, media, and other society institutions to disseminate the orders to the masses. This is not a political issue. This is not a one-party-against-the-other issue. This has affected everybody. I don't care your color. I don't care your ethnicity. I don't care your political views. This should raise questions in your mind.

Before moving on to the next subject, I want to state one more quote from the Johns Hopkins Event 201 web page that was included in a "statement of clarification" regarding their pandemic exercise:

"For the scenario, we modeled a fictional Coronavirus pandemic, but we explicitly stated that it was not a prediction. Instead, the exercise served to highlight preparedness and response challenges that would likely arise in a very severe pandemic. We are not now predicting that the nCoV-2019 outbreak will kill 65 million people. Although our tabletop exercise included a mock novel Coronavirus, the inputs we used for modeling the potential impact of that fictional virus are not similar to nCoV-2019."[138]

The Event 201 took place in October 2019, and according to a report at TheGurardian.com, the first cases of Covid hit China in November

---

137. Centerforhealthsecurity.org, Johns Hopkins Center for Health Security, Event 201 Pandemic Tabletop Exercise, https://centerforhealthsecurity.org/our-work/tabletop-exercises/event-201-pandemic-tabletop-exercise.

138. Centerforhealthsecurity.org, Johns Hopkins Bloomberg School of Public Health, Statement about nCoV and our pandemic exercise (Johns Hopkins, orig. published Jan. 2020), https://centerforhealthsecurity.org/2020/statement-about-ncov-and-our-pandemic-exercise-0.

2019, just weeks after the "high-level pandemic exercise."[139]

I found another source that backs up my theory that this entire pandemic dress rehearsal was not organic. A friend brought something interesting to my attention. Journalist Harry Vox appeared in a television interview in 2014 that pointed to a report he discovered called "Scenarios for the Future of Technology and International Development" that was published in May 2010 by The Rockefeller Foundation and the Global Business Network. The report has a section titled: "Lock Step: Scenario Narratives." It basically describes a scenario similar to what we experienced with the pandemic, even including China in the outline.

In my opinion, this is a propaganda piece they released in 2010 almost 10 years earlier to get the masses mentally ready for coming events. In the report, they tried to cloak the scenarios as something for the public good, to help make societies more resilient and able to bounce back from unexpected circumstances. They go as far as to say that, "scenarios are not predictions." Maybe they are not predictions, but this scenario could have been from one of the great prophets and have been spot on, down to mask wearing and body temperature checks that you get at the dental office today.

This report does not try to hide the fact that they are looking to spawn an authoritarian police state worldwide and using events such as the pandemic to reach their goals.

The following text is from the Rockefeller report on page 18. Pay close attention to the similarity to our real-world pandemic event. As of this writing, you can still find multiple downloads of the report online.

Remember, this is also a supposed mock scenario.

---

139. TheGuardian.com, First Covid-19 case happened in November, China government records show, https://www.theguardian.com/world/2020/mar/13/first-covid-19-case-happened-in-november-china-government-records-show-report.

## Scenario Narratives

## Lock Step

"A world of tighter top-down government control and more authoritarian leadership, with limited innovation and growing citizen pushback."[140]

So we are supposed to be quiet and take orders from the "authoritarian leadership"? Let's see what else they had planned ...

> In 2012, the pandemic that the world had been anticipating for years finally hit. Unlike 2009's H1N1, this new influenza strain—originating from wild geese—was extremely virulent and deadly. Even the most pandemic-prepared nations were quickly overwhelmed when the virus streaked around the world, infecting nearly 20 percent of the global population and killing 8 million in just seven months, the majority of them healthy young adults. The pandemic also had a deadly effect on economies: international mobility of both people and goods screeched to a halt, debilitating industries like tourism and breaking global supply chains. Even locally, normally bustling shops and office buildings sat empty for months, devoid of both employees and customers.[141]

The Covid pandemic did stop commerce dead in its tracks globally, and we still see supply chain disruptions as of this writing. The scenario continues:

> The pandemic blanketed the planet—though disproportionate numbers died in Africa, Southeast Asia, and Central America, where the virus spread like wildfire in the absence of official

140. Nommeraadio.ee, Scenarios for the Future of Technology and International Development, The Rockefeller Foundation and Global Business Network, May 2010, pg. 18 https://www.nommeraadio.ee/meedia/pdf/RRS/Rockefeller%20Foundation.pdf.

141. Nommeraadio.ee, Scenarios for the Future of Technology and International Development, The Rockefeller Foundation and Global Business Network, May 2010, p. 18, https://www.nommeraadio.ee/meedia/pdf/RRS/Rockefeller%20Foundation.pdf.

containment protocols. But even in developed countries, containment was a challenge. The United States' initial policy of "strongly discouraging" citizens from flying proved deadly in its leniency, accelerating the spread of the virus not just within the U.S. but across borders. However, a few countries did fare better—China in particular. The Chinese government's quick imposition and enforcement of mandatory quarantine for all citizens, as well as its instant and near-hermetic sealing off of all borders, saved millions of lives, stopping the spread of the virus far earlier than in other countries and enabling a swifter post-pandemic recovery.[142]

And here, China is the hero, the good guy—they did everything right. The pinnacle of pandemic control perfection.

"China's government was not the only one that took extreme measures to protect its citizens from risk and exposure. During the pandemic, national leaders around the world flexed their authority and imposed airtight rules and restrictions, from the mandatory wearing of face masks to body-temperature checks at the entries to communal spaces like train stations and supermarkets."[143]

Let's see what happens to our freedoms in this continuing drama. They plan to use the pandemic to rule with an iron fist from here forward. Once you give up a few freedoms, don't expect them back!

"Even after the pandemic faded, this more authoritarian control and oversight of citizens and their activities stuck and even intensified. In order to protect themselves from the spread of increasingly global problems—from pandemics and transnational terrorism to environmental crises and

---

142. Ibid.
143. Ibid, p. 19.

rising poverty—leaders around the world took a firmer grip on power."[144]

Although this report has couched this event as a 'mock' scenario, notice how eerily similar it is to our reality regarding Covid-19. Did you catch that? "Even after the pandemic faded, this more authoritarian control and oversight of citizens and their activities stuck and even intensified." This was my fear all along regarding our real-life scenario. They present the problem, they swoop in with the solution, and they use the event to further their control tactics.

This narrative holds up China, a tyrannical government, as a model the U.S. should use if ever they find themselves in this type of pandemic scenario—and like magic, it happened ten years later.

Unfortunately, if we as a people go along with these tactics and don't stand up for our rights, there is no going back to our *normal* way of life. We keep hearing about the *new normal*. I fear this is our fate and that is exactly what they want from us—fear and compliance with their *new normal* in a New World Order.

So the $64,000 question is: Did they know what was coming? Was Event 201 the dress rehearsal before the live show? Use your critical thinking skills.

In the next section, I'll describe the players in this production.

## Event 201 – The Players

We know the major stars of the Event 201 were Johns Hopkins University, the Gates Foundation, and the World Economic Forum.

I touched briefly on the World Economic Forum and their tentacles into major financial, medical, educational, business, government, and other world institutions. The Event 201 pandemic exercise included a

---

144. Nommeraadio.ee, Scenarios for the Future of Technology and International Development, The Rockefeller Foundation and Global Business Network, May 2010, pg. 19 https://www.nommeraadio.ee/meedia/pdf/RRS/Rockefeller%20Foundation.pdf.

cast of characters from a variety of these areas of society worldwide. Many can be found on the Event 201 website under the appropriately named section, "Players."

I will not name these players individually because you probably would not recognize them; you can easily find their names on the Event 201 website. However, I will list a few by company name or institution name and title to drive my point home regarding public/private partnerships and their roles in carrying out the narrative and orders from the global elite.

In addition to media, these were some of the role players that took to the stage for Event 201:

Marriott International

United Nations Foundation

Henry Scheins U.S. Medical Group

Gates Foundation, Global Development Program President

ANZ Bank (Australian), board member and also ironically the chairman of Coalition for Epidemic Preparedness and Innovation

McGill University, Asso. Dean of School of Population and Global Health

Chinese CDC, Dir. General

Johns Hopkins University, Sr. Research Fellow

Edelman Communications firm

Lufthansa Group, Sr. Dir. Head of Crisis Emergency and Business Continuity Mgt.

CDC, Deputy Dir. Public Health Service and Implementation Science

Johnson & Johnson, VP Global Public Health

UPS Foundation, President [145]

---

145. Centerforhealthsecurity.org, Johns Hopkins Bloomberg School of Public Health, Event 201, Players https://centerforhealthsecurity.org/our-work/tabletop-exercises/event-201-pandemic-tabletop-exercise#players.

# My Thoughts on Event 201

I certainly do not think Event 201 was a coincidence that just happened to precede the Covid reality facing us on a worldwide scale today. My Spidey senses tell me the Event 201 was a dress rehearsal for the real-life stage show we experienced across the world.

In my opinion, and of course I can be wrong, I think Event 201 brought many institutions, businesses, media, and other important players together to write the script outline of what had to play out once the show started to occur in real time.

This pandemic has resulted in major societal changes across the board and across the world. Many have been planned by the global elitists for decades. Some of these factors include: population control, surveillance society, food control, monetary control, gun control, and even movement from state to state.

I am not making this up. This is what I discovered while researching Event 201. I am just putting together pieces that I found during research to build my case. Whether it turns out that I am right or wrong—I want to alert people that this Event 201 did indeed take place just before the pandemic transpired, and I think this is a very important fact to ponder.

Before we even heard of Coronavirus, the cast of characters was already knee deep in this. So this was not something new. It was new to us. We had never heard of Coronavirus, this big, scary monster that we could not see. But there are many connections between the global elites, their foundations, big corporations, and what is going on now. We're going to look at them and follow the money. So of course, I'm going to start with the Gates Foundation.

# Follow the Leader and You'll Find the Money

*(Gates Foundation, Pirbright, and Fauci)*

Since Bill Gates took center stage throughout the Coronavirus pandemic and was seemingly hell bent on coming up with the vaccine solution, it is only natural that I would start looking at his foundation, their partners, monies that may have changed hands, and projects they have been involved in.

I know that many believe Bill Gates is involved in the development process of a Coronavirus vaccine because he is a philanthropist and wants to save people. I don't believe this. In my opinion, he has a lot to gain monetarily. I cannot prove what is in his heart. I can only reveal the ties I have found between him and the big players in the vaccine game. It is up to people to make their own decisions about Gates.

Another simple fact to make my point can be found on Forbes lists. In 2010, Forbes listed Bill Gates as the "richest man in America," and his net worth was $54 billion.[146]

After a project he created called "Decade of Vaccines," whose mission was to vaccinate the world between 2010 and 2020, CNBC published his new net worth 11 years later—as of December 2021—and he had more than doubled his wealth to $139 billion.[147]

He is not new to the vaccine game. He has been in it for decades—gaining a lot of power and making a lot of money.

As Bill Gates retired from the Microsoft board, he almost simultaneously thrust himself into Covid-19.

During my research, I stumbled onto articles that claimed the Bill and

---

146. Money.com, Forbes 400 Richest Americans https://money.cnn.com/2010/09/22/news/companies/forbes_400/index.htm.

147. CNBC.com, The world's 10 richest people added $402 billion to their fortunes in 2021. Here's whose net worth grew the most, by Nicolas Vega, Dec. 30, 2021, https://www.cnbc.com/2021/12/30/how-much-money-the-10-richest-people-in-the-world-made-in-2021.html.

Melinda Gates Foundation had ties to the Pirbright Institute that held several Coronavirus-related patents. I wanted to find out for myself if this was true and what the connection might be between Gates and Pirbright. What did they have in common? Here is what I found.

## Pirbright—Stop One

First, I went to the Pirbright Institute website to find out what they do. According to their website, they are located in Pirbright, Woking, Great Britain. One of the first things that caught my eye was a section called, "Viruses We Study." This is what it states, "The list below contains the diseases we work on … for example, bluetongue virus (BTV) and African horse sickness (AHS) along with epizootic hemorrhagic disease virus (EHDV) all belong to the Reoviridae family, and infectious bronchitis virus (IBV) is within the Coronavirus family."[148]

Of course, "Coronavirus family" stood out right away. But the other thing that stood out was "infectious bronchitis virus" or what they call IBV. The reason is that the website says it affects the respiratory system, which is one of the fatal symptoms experienced by victims of Covid-19. I will talk more about IBV later.

According to the Pirbright website, these are their mission and values: "… a world leading center of excellence in research and surveillance of virus diseases of farm animals and viruses that spread from animals to humans. We receive strategic funding from the Biotechnology and Biological Sciences Research Council … apply scientific research to prevent and control viral diseases, protecting animal and human health and the economy."[149]

There are two major points to take note of in this paragraph, and I will demonstrate later why they are important.

---

148. Pirbright.ac.uk, Our Science, Viruses We Study, https://www.pirbright.ac.uk/viruses-we-study.

149. Pirbright.ac.uk, About Us, Mission and Values, https://www.pirbright.ac.uk/about-us/our-mission-values.

1) They say they do research on viruses from farm animals and viruses that spread from animals to humans.

2) They say their vision is to control viral diseases, protecting animals and human health and the economy (not only animal health, but human health).

These points will be very important as we take a look at the patents.

## The Pirbright Patents

Next I went to the U.S. Patent and Trademark Office website to find out if there was truth to the patent claim. I punched in "Pirbright," and nineteen results were assigned to them.

The first entry was patent number 10130701, titled, "Coronavirus." The names of three people are listed as the "inventors." A litany of dates in the patent record went back as far as October 2004. I am not sure what that means, but the date on the Coronavirus patent is November 20, 2018, and the application file date is shown as January 23, 2015. So Pirbright received a Coronavirus-related patent one year before we see the first cases start to show up in real life in China.

Here is the exact text on the patent document that appears under "Abstract":

"The present invention provides a live, attenuated Coronavirus comprising a variant replicase gene encoding polyproteins comprising a mutation in one or more of non-structural protein(s) (nsp)-10, nsp-14, nsp-15 or nsp-16. The Coronavirus may be used as a vaccine for treating and/or preventing a disease, such as infectious bronchitis, in a subject."[150]

Note that the paragraph above does not specifically mention that this is only related to livestock research. It states a "vaccine for treating and/or preventing a disease, such as infectious bronchitis, in a subject." A subject

---

150. U.S. Patent and Trademark Office, Coronavirus, US-10130701-B2,
https://image-ppubs.uspto.gov/dirsearch-public/print/downloadPdf/10130701.

could refer to either an animal or a human.

Further down the page on the patent document listed under "Field of the Invention" this text appears: "The present invention relates to an attenuated Coronavirus comprising a variant replicase gene, which causes the virus to have reduced pathogenicity. The present invention also relates to the use of such a Coronavirus in a vaccine to prevent and/or treat a disease."[151]

Note that neither statement says this is only for research with animals or livestock. That being said, under the heading, "Background to the Invention," a substantial amount of text is dedicated to *avian* (bird) references. But under a section labeled, "Detailed Description," there is a mix of references to mammals, birds, human coronaviruses, livestock, domesticated pets, bovine, porcine, rats, and more.

The other interesting patent I found from Pirbright had to do with the "infectious bronchitis virus (IBV)." It would seem that a bronchitis virus would be a common thread between the Covid patent and possibly the IBV patent since many people hospitalized for Covid have experienced breathing or respiratory problems. The Pirbright Institute filed for patents related to these two conditions, one was a Coronavirus-related patent and one was an infectious-bronchitis virus-related patent.

The patent number for the IBV is 9969777 and was issued to the Pirbright Institute on May 15, 2018. Ironically, this patent title uses a term we have heard repeatedly that is seemingly a classic characteristic of the Coronavirus, "spike protein."

The title of the IBV patent is listed as, "Mutant spike protein extending the tissue tropism of infectious bronchitis (IBV)."[152]

---

151. Ibid.

152. U.S. Patent and Trademark Office, Mutant spike protein extending the tissue tropism of infectious bronchitis (IBV), US-9969777-B2, https://image-ppubs.uspto.gov/dirsearch-public/print/downloadPdf/9969777.

Not being a physician or familiar with medical terms, I looked up "tissue tropism." It means cells and tissues of a host support the growth of a particular virus or bacteria. So does the title mean that once a mutant spike protein is in the body, it will enhance or support the growth of that particular virus or bacteria?

An illustration of what I mean would be that the Coronavirus is the "vehicle" that carries the spike protein, and the spike protein is the "engine" that ignites the body into the virus state. Keeping this in mind: These two patents were coincidentally issued to the institute in close proximity—within six months.

If the spike protein is the "engine," it was granted first in May 2018. Then the "vehicle" that carries the "engine" was granted in November 2018. Is this truly a coincidence? Common sense tells me it could have been intentional. Of course, I have no proof of this. Everything I am writing regarding Pirbright and these patents is pure speculation. To be fair, this is just my opinion.

Here is the timeline of the filings and issuance of the two patents:

May 2014 – Spike protein-related patent was filed.

January 2015 – Coronavirus-related patent was filed.

May 2018 - Spike protein-related patent was issued.

November 2018 – Coronavirus-related patent was issued.

Here is the text that appears on the IBV patent document listed under Field of the Invention: "The present invention relates to a Coronavirus spike protein (S protein). In particular an IBV S protein which, when used to produce a virus, causes the virus to have extended tissue tropism. The present invention also relates to nucleotide sequences encoding such an S protein; viral particles comprising such an S protein and their use in a vaccine to prevent and/or treat a disease."[153]

Again, take note that the statement does not specify 'for animal research only.' But to make sure I cover all bases, again, under the "Background to the Invention" section, it primarily references birds.

A quote I discovered from *The Daily Caller* suggests there might be some truth to the possibility I outlined above regarding the spike protein. In December of 2019, Peter Daszak, president of Ecohealth, made the following comment,

"You can manipulate them in the lab pretty easily," Daszak said. "Spike protein drives a lot of what happens with the Coronavirus. *Zoonotic risk*. So you can get the sequence, you can build the protein—and we work with Ralph Baric at [the University of North Carolina] to do this—and insert the backbone of another virus and do some work in the lab."[154]

Daszak admits the following:

Spike proteins can be manipulated in a lab.

Spike proteins drive a lot of what happens in Coronavirus.

You can get the sequence and build the protein.

This is being done this at the University of North Carolina.

They can insert the backbone of another virus in the lab.

Daszak stated that "spike proteins" are instrumental in how Coronavirus acts.

When I looked up the meaning of *Zoonotic risk*, the meaning is, "… any disease or infection that is naturally transmissible from vertebrate animals to humans." [155]

---

153. Ibid.

154. The Daily Caller, US Scientist With Close Ties To Wuhan Lab Discussed Manipulating Bat-Based Coronaviruses Just Weeks Before Outbreak, Andrew Kerr, January 2021, https://dailycaller.com/2021/01/21/peter-daszak-manipulating-Coronavirus-interview/.

155. Search.yahoo.com, https://search.yahoo.com/search?fr=mcafee&type=E211US105G91647&p=what+is+Zoonotic+risk

Is it coincidence that Pirbright was working on a "spike protein" patent and received it just 1.5 years before the real-life pandemic? Again, I want to reiterate that this is speculation on my part, but if you look at the patterns of planning that were revealed through Event 201, one must wonder: Is all of this a coincidence?

## Pirbright Partnerships

To research more about the Gates connection to Pirbright and their other partners, I went to a page called Partnerships, and then to a section titled, "Major Stakeholders." At the top of this page, there was an obvious statement in bold letters. It was a disclaimer that clearly pointed out an edit had been made to the original published page. It was purposely put there to get attention, and in my opinion, to put questions in the reader's mind. Here is exactly what the disclaimer says on the website:

"Edited: 7 May 2020. The Pirbright Institute is aware that misinformation regarding the Institute and its research is circulating on social media following the Covid-19 outbreak. The facts regarding our Coronavirus research and funding can be found in this statement."[156]

So anybody seeing this would immediately assume that *misinformation* must have been circulating on social media about Pirbright, their research, and funding.

The link to the "statement" about the "misinformation" then brought one to another page that had this headline: "Pirbright's Livestock Coronavirus Research—your questions answered."

Before a reader would go further, this headline gives the impression that Pirbright's Coronavirus research specifically dealt with livestock.

Here is the exact statement they issued regarding the information they claim is "misinformation":

---

156. The Pirbright Institute, Partnerships, Our Major Stakeholders, https://www.pirbright.ac.uk/partnerships/our-major-stakeholders.

The Pirbright Institute is aware that misinformation regarding the Institute and its research is circulating on social media following an outbreak of a new (novel) Coronavirus that infects humans in Wuhan, China. These are the facts regarding our Coronavirus research and funding.

The Pirbright Institute carries out research on infectious bronchitis virus (IBV), a Coronavirus that infects poultry, and porcine delta Coronavirus that infects pigs. Pirbright does not currently work with human Coronaviruses. More information on our Coronavirus livestock research can be found on our website.

The Institute holds Patent no. 10130701 which covers the development of an attenuated (weakened) form of the Coronavirus that could potentially be used as a vaccine to prevent respiratory diseases in birds and other animals. Many vaccines are made in this way, from flu to polio. We have not yet developed an IBV vaccine, but research is ongoing.

The Institute is strategically funded by the Biotechnology and Biological Sciences Research Council, part of UK Research and Innovation (BBSRC UKRI) and also receives funding from many other organisations including the Bill & Melinda Gates Foundation. The patented work was not funded by the Bill & Melinda Gates Foundation. More information on The Livestock Antibody Hub which is funded by the Bill & Melinda Gates Foundation is available on our website.[157]

People must have started to draw conclusions that Pirbright's Coronavirus patent was related to human virus research. So they went out of their way to create a special statement page to negate and in my opinion to diffuse these conclusions. Let's revisit the statement and look

157. The Pirbright Institute, Pirbright's livestock coronavirus research – your questions answered, Jan. 2020, https://www.pirbright.ac.uk/news/2020/01/pirbright%E2%80%99s-livestock-coronavirus-research -%E2%80%93-your-questions-answered.

at two glaring pieces. "Pirbright does not currently work with human Coronaviruses ... many vaccines are made in this way, from flu to polio. We have not yet developed an IBV vaccine, but research is ongoing."[158]

This statement insinuates that the patent I found on Coronavirus has nothing to do with the human Coronavirus. Notice it says, "not currently." It does not say they will never use this research for the human virus type. Their Coronavirus patent document does state in section 46, "The vaccine or vaccine composition of the invention may be used to treat a human, animal, or avian subject.", and the abstract statement refers to a "subject." This does not mean it is *not* for animals, but I am saying that it is left open to interpretation regarding humans, and I think this is on purpose. What would be the reason for this?

The statement also says, "We have not yet developed an IBV vaccine, but research is ongoing." This statement also does not mean "never." It means *not currently*.

Remember, I called attention to two major points on the Pirbright website earlier? Let's review them here:

1) They say they research viruses from farm animals and viruses that spread from animals to humans.
2) They say their vision is to control viral diseases, to protect animals, human health and the economy.

Do these two points sound like they will never dabble in human virus research? That is impossible if you are researching viruses that spread from animals to humans, or if you say your vision is to control viral diseases, protecting animals and human health.

Even if you start research with animals and your goal is to protect human health, at some point the research has to include humans, doesn't it?

_____

158. Ibid.

Another point I want to bring to your attention is that this entity made a name change in October of 2012. Formerly, they were known as the Institute for Animal Health. They changed the name to the Pirbright Institute. Here is an excerpt from the press release they published on their website regarding the name change in 2012. "The Institute will continue to carry out its world leading surveillance and research into virus diseases of livestock and viruses that spread from animals to humans. It will have the facilities and expertise to meet the known and emerging virus threats of the 21st century."[159]

In my opinion, once again, when they speak about viruses that spread from animals to humans, this could be left open to interpretation about whether or not their work includes human research. Yet Pirbright states repeatedly on their website that they work with livestock viruses. In my opinion, they're really trying to convince you that any of their current research has nothing to do with the human form of the Coronavirus, but is primarily with animals. I cannot prove that this is or is not the case. I believe you can look at the facts and read between the lines. And just because they currently are not researching humans, does that mean they will *never* research humans?

Your response might be, so what? So what if they are dealing with the human form of the virus? What difference does it make? In my opinion, since there is a connection between the Gates Foundation and Pirbright, and if there is a human virus research connection, this would point to that fact that someone would gain monetarily from successful vaccine research. But the bigger question is: Why would they hide the human virus research? If you are philanthropic, why hide this important work and try to convince visitors to the website that there is no connection here?

---

159. The Pirbright Institute, News, A new identity, Oct. 2012, https://www.pirbright.ac.uk/node/356.

# The Gates Pirbright Connection (and funding)

As I mentioned earlier, the Bill & Melinda Gates Foundation is listed as a "major stakeholder" on the Pirbright website.

Pirbright makes a big deal about the connection between the Institute and the Gates Foundation—so much so that they dedicated an entire section to debunking negative questions that anybody might have, as it relates to Coronavirus, the Gates Foundation, and their Institute. Why? It is my opinion that they do not want people to think that the money they've received from the Gates Foundations has anything to do with the human Coronavirus.

Pirbright says on its website that the Coronavirus patent was not funded by the Bill & Melinda Gates Foundation. However, in November 2019, just as China was seeing their first cases of Coronavirus, Pirbright announced a livestock antibody research project that was awarded $5.5 million by the Gates Foundation. The announcement regarding the project states that, " … This is aimed at improving animal and human health globally."[160]

You are probably saying that doesn't prove anything, and you are right; it does not. But I think it is strange that just as the pandemic real-life scenario is about to begin on a worldwide scale, both of these entities are up to their ears in a project where the research according to their own words, "will be used to drive vaccine selection and design and test antibody therapies … which will improve animal health and ultimately human health… ,"[161] and that oh, by the way, Coronavirus vaccine and antibody therapies were both released to the public shortly thereafter for a worldwide Coronavirus pandemic.

---

160. The Pirbright Institute, News, Bill & Melinda Gates Foundation funds development of Pirbright's Livestock Antibody Hub supporting animal and human health, https://www.pirbright.ac.uk/news/2019/11/bill-melinda-gates-foundation-funds-development-pirbright%E2%80%99s-livestock-antibody-hub.
161. Ibid.

Maybe that's not initially what the money was allocated for, but could it indirectly, down the line, go toward anything leading to Coronavirus human research? And yet, if you use your brain and can read between the lines, or have an opinion, or ask questions, you are spreading misinformation.

I'm trying to make connections regarding what they're claiming versus what they're really doing. I'm saying that I don't necessarily buy what they are saying.

This is the connection between Gates and Pirbright. From 2013 to 2021, the Pirbright Institute received well over $21.5 million in funding for a variety of things that include foot-and-mouth, antibodies, seed viruses, and influenza vaccine.

There's obviously a connection here—a high dollar connection. My assessment, which is purely speculative regarding their relationship, is that it is a lot more about money than philanthropy.

The reason for my research on this topic was to try to reveal some things you probably were not aware of and encourage you to think critically about the information presented to you so that you can make up your own mind!

## Fauci and Gates Connection

What is Fauci's connection to the Gates Foundation? How long have they been working together? What is their history?

During the daily pandemic news conferences, rumors flew in the press that there had been a longstanding relationship between the then (and now former) Director of the National Institute of Allergy and Infectious Diseases (NIAID), Anthony Fauci, and at that point in time according to their Wikipedia entry, " … is one of the 27 institutes and centers that make up the National Institutes of Health (NIH)."[162]

As part of the National Institutes of Health, Fauci, "oversaw an extensive research portfolio of basic and applied research to prevent, diagnose, and treat established infectious diseases such as HIV/AIDS, respiratory infections, diarrheal diseases, tuberculosis, and malaria as well as emerging diseases such as Ebola, Zika, and Covid-19. He also led the NIAID research effort on transplantation and immune-related illnesses, including autoimmune disorders, asthma, and allergies."[163]

Before the pandemic was top of mind, Fauci and Gates were united in other projects. Fauci served on the Scientific Board of the Bill & Melinda Gates Foundation for their Global Grand Challenges from 2003-2010.[164]

Fauci was appointed to the Leadership Council of a Gates Foundation project dating back to 2010 called Decade of Vaccines (which I mentioned earlier). This program received $10 billion from the Gates Foundation.

The purpose of the Decades of Vaccines project was to bring vaccines to the world. "Bill and Melinda Gates announced today that their foundation will commit $10 billion over the next 10 years to help research, develop and deliver vaccines for the world's poorest countries ... Bill and Melinda Gates made their announcement at the World Economic Forum's Annual Meeting, where they were joined by Julian Lob-Levyt, CEO of the GAVI Alliance."[165]

The GAVI Alliance was created in 1999 by the Gates Foundation, in my opinion, to help push the vaccine agenda worldwide.

What does GAVI do? According to their website, GAVI, the Vaccine

---

162. Wikipedia.com, National Institute of Allergy and Infectious Diseases, https://en.wikipedia.org/wiki/National_Institute_of_Allergy_and_Infectious_Diseases.

163. National Institutes of Allergy and Infectious Diseases, Former NIAID Director, https://www.niaid.nih.gov/about/director.

164. Global Grand Challenges, Scientific Board, https://gcgh.grandchallenges.org/about/scientific-board.

165. Gates Foundation, Leadership Council, Decade of Vaccines, https://www.gatesfoundation.org/Ideas/Media-Center/Press-Releases/2010/12/Global-Health-Leaders-Launch-Decade-of-Vaccines-Collaboration.

Alliance, has the following purpose: " … Gavi is an international organisation—a global Vaccine Alliance, bringing together public and private sectors with the shared goal of saving lives and protecting people's health by increasing equitable and sustainable use of vaccines."[166]

Fauci has another connection to Gates through GAVI. In a 2012 interview, Fauci said he wanted the NIH to work closer with GAVI, "…if you look at the spectrum, you, GAVI, develop a vaccine and get it into the arms of people who need them. We, NIH, work on the upstream component of the fundamental research development."[167]

Fauci is saying that the NIH work would naturally dovetail with the GAVI Alliances's vaccine development and distribution work.

These are just some of the connections I found on the websites of organizations that seem to play a big part in planning, development, and distribution of vaccines; the connections are undeniable.

## Wrap Up Coincidences

The Gates Foundation that hosted the pandemic simulation was then involved in a race to help get the vaccine for Coronavirus distributed worldwide. Their world partners include: World Health Organization, UNICEF, the World Bank, and GAVI.

GAVI approved a five-year strategy (2021-2025) "to leave no one behind" in terms of worldwide immunization. Is it coincidence that all of these partners are playing integral parts in the pandemic? Could it be the pandemic has helped them with their "Decade of Vaccines" agenda?

Is it also a coincidence that the same people who are worried about your health are also investing in vaccine research and trying to get these vaccines to market?

---

166. GAVI.org, About GAVI, https://www.gavi.org/our-alliance/about.
167. GAVI.org, Fauci: forging closer ties with GAVI, May 2012, https://www.gavi.org/news/media-room/fauci-forging-closer-ties-gavi.

Is it totally out of the goodness of their hearts?

GAVI has what they call an innovative finance mechanism. It is a matching fund used to attract money for their immunization programs. The GAVI website states, "The Gavi Matching Fund multiplies private sector partners' impact by doubling their investment ... , a public-private funding mechanism designed to incentivise private sector investments in immunisation."[168]

Did you notice that they use the word *investment,* not *donate?* Why would you invest money? Because you expect a return on your investment, right? You're putting out money in hopes that you're going to make a return. This isn't just philanthropic. Although they want to cloak themselves in philanthropy, the truth is, they're investing in these vaccine programs to make money.

Here are more players in the vaccine game who made a lot of money off of this pandemic.

## Follow the Money, Big Pharma Makes Billions

According to Robert F. Kennedy Jr.'s book, *The Real Anthony Fauci,* as Americans lost their jobs and wealth due to lockdowns and business shutdowns, many of those in elite circles of business, technology, and pharmaceuticals made billions of dollars individually and trillions collectively.

"In 2020, workers lost $3.7 trillion while billionaires gained $3.9 trillion. Some 493 individuals became new billionaires, and an additional 8 million Americans dropped below the poverty line."[169]

Kennedy goes on to say those who made big money are in Big Technology, Big Data, Big Telecom, Big Finance, Big Media—and names

---

168. GAVI.org, The Gavi Matching Fund
https://www.gavi.org/investing-gavi/innovative-financing/gavi-matching-fund.
169. *The Real Anthony Fauci: Bill Gates, Big Pharma, and the Global War on Democracy and Public Health* by Robert F. Kennedy, Jr. (Children's Health Defense) November 16, 2021, p. 34-35.

some of those that gained wealth during lockdowns.

Michael Bloomberg, $7 billion;

Bill Gates, $22 billion;

Jeff Bezos, $86 billion;

Sergey Brin, $41 billion;

Mark Zuckerberg, $35 billion;

Larry Ellison, $34 billion.

According to a Forbes.com's report, in 2021, a record 493 new billionaires joined the Forbes' World's Billionaires list. "*…at least 40 new entrants who draw their fortunes from companies involved in fighting Covid-19…*thanks to vaccines they helped develop. Others got rich making everything from personal protective equipment and diagnostic test to antibody treatments…"[170]

Here are just a few listed on the report and their net worth:

Stéphane Bancel - Moderna's CEO (net worth $4.3 billion)

Ugur Sahin - CEO and co-founder of BioNTech (net worth $4 billion)

Timothy Springer - an immunologist and founding investor of Moderna (net worth $2.2 billion)

Noubar Afeyan - Moderna's Chairman (net worth $1.9 billion)

Sergio Stevanato – Stevanato Group Chairman, medical packaging (net worth $1.9 billion)

Juan Lopez-Belmonte - Chairman of ROVI, a company with a deal to manufacture and package the Moderna vaccine (net worth $1.8 billion)

170. Forbes.com, Meet The 40 New Billionaires Who Got Rich Fighting Covid-19, Giacomo Tognini, April 2021,https://www.forbes.com/sites/giacomotognini/2021/04/06/meet-the-40-new-billionaires-who-got-rich-fighting-covid-19/?sh=669ce9ea17e5

Robert Langer - a scientist and founding investor in Moderna
(net worth $1.6 billion)[171]

I've talked enough about the pandemic partnerships, funding, patents, and connections. I think you get the picture I'm trying to paint. I want to end the Pandemic Chronicles with information regarding the mask. I believe the mask has been a "purposeful" prop in the entire pandemic production—both in the physical and spiritual realms.

## The Masks—What You Should Know

My natural reaction is one of resistance when it comes to wearing the mask. I am not one to follow the herd—I've always had what many would term a *stubborn streak*. I call it *free thinking, critical thinking,* or *thinking for myself.* I wholly respect and understand real, non-corrupt authority and its importance in life. God created it for order. Without it there would not have been a civilized American society. It could have been total chaos.

Where am I going with this? The mask. During this pandemic scare, we were told to wear a mask, and in some cases we were forced, for our safety and the safety of others. I believe it had nothing to do with preserving human health, but everything to do with control. Law-abiding Americans who didn't want to wear a mask in a "supposed free country" were demonized. In my experience, those on the political left seemed to be pushing law-abiding citizens to wear masks; yet they had nothing to say to lawless people as they went across the nation in packs vandalizing business and personal property. Where was the outcry to preserve human health? These law breakers did not use the "social distancing" precautions that the politically left so readily pontificated.

Because I was hearing more and more about some municipalities across

171. Forbes.com, Meet The 40 New Billionaires Who Got Rich Fighting Covid-19, Giacomo Tognini, April 2021,https://www.forbes.com/sites/giacomotognini/2021/04/06/meet-the-40-new-billionaires-who-got-rich-fighting-covid-19/?sh=669ce9ea17e5.

the country mandating mask wearing, I decided to look into two areas surrounding this idea.

1) Is it constitutional to mandate mask wearing? I am guessing it is counter to the Fourth Amendment under our Bill of Rights.

2) Common sense tells me that wearing a mask cannot be good if one is cutting off the fresh air (oxygen) breathed in (especially when trying to preserve a strong immune system to fight the virus), while re-breathing the carbon dioxide expelled when breathing out, and doing this over and over again for an extended period of time. This seems like insane behavior to me.

The other irony concerns those who claim the "high levels" of CO2 in the air cause "climate change." The CO2 trapped under the mask is breathed over and over again.

Unless of course, that is the point—to keep levels of CO2 in the atmosphere down, while making people sick from re-breathing that same "toxic CO2" (their words).

I am not a doctor, but this is common sense.

Dr. Russell Blaylock is a doctor. He has been treating patients for decades, unlike Dr. Fauci. He is an M.D. and here is what he states regarding viruses and wearing a mask—and it dovetails with what I called *common sense.*

"By wearing a mask, the exhaled viruses will not be able to escape and will concentrate in the nasal passages, enter the olfactory nerves and travel into the brain."[172]

Before the pandemic brought mask-wearing to the forefront of life on a worldwide scale, studies and published reports revealed how masks could affect healthcare professionals in surgical theatres. The following finding showed a decrease in blood oxygen levels.

---

172. Blaylock: Face Masks Pose Serious Risks To The Healthy https://ratical.org/PandemicParallaxView/ Blaylock-MaskPoseSeriousRisks.pdf?fbclid=IwAR07iNoX78HD9W4x0vRm6sZTOiWrkz8tcwwsh 5PM_oeP2X4bwh67U-053W4.

## Study on Wearing Masks in Surgical Theatres

While researching the topic on prolonged mask wearing, I stumbled onto a blog post from June 2017, years before this issue came up in our everyday lives. The concern was in relation to re-breathing $CO_2$, and the physical effects as it relates to bag breathing. To be clear, the writer's intent was *not* to discourage mask wearing, but to see if it would be an alternative to bag breathing when hyperventilating, as those having a panic attack might do.

The post titled, "Surgical Masks Increase Pulse, Lower Oxygen Saturation from Rebreathing $CO_2$," directed readers to a preliminary report on surgical mask-induced deoxygenation when performing surgery.

The report highlighted in the blog post is called, "Preliminary report on surgical mask induced deoxygenation during major surgery." Following are a couple of excerpts from that report.

> Although decrease in both mental - physical performance and accuracy may sometimes be overcome by the motivation of the surgeon, increased fatigue is common in lengthy operations. The increased endogenous heat production of the surgeon, as well as many aspects of the operating room situation - even the close environment beneath the surgical mask - may also negatively affect the working condition of the surgeon.

> Surgical masks may impose some measurable airway resistance, but it seems doubtful if this significantly increases the process of breathing. Although it might have appeared to be likely that hypoxemia results from the increased $CO_2$ content of the inspired air due to the exhaled $CO_2$ getting trapped beneath the surgical face mask; there has been no controlled study concerning with the effect of surgical masks on the level of blood oxygenation.

> In this study we have measured the oxygen saturation of arterial pulsations (SpO2) by a pulse oximeter and found a statistically significant decrease in the blood O2 saturation level of the surgeons post operationally, which is not due to prolonged standing or stress.[173]

The purpose of the study was to learn whether or not surgeons' oxygen saturation of hemoglobin was affected by the surgical mask during major operations.

The outcome showed lower oxygen saturation levels and higher pulse rates, especially in participants over thirty-five years old.

It could be argued that these physical limitations could affect a surgeon's performance in the surgical theatre, especially for procedures taking longer periods of time. I believe the mask has nothing to do with the mainstream-touted narrative wrapped around health concerns. I believe a much more sinister reason reaches the spiritual realm.

## What is the Mask Really About?

Over the course of the pandemic, all media showed more and more images of people wearing masks. They said it was to keep people safe from the deadly Covid-19 pandemic. If you watched the images being presented by all forms of media, whether TV news anchors, public service announcements, web advertisements for the latest "fashion" in masks— you couldn't deny the very hard push for everyone to wear a mask.

A variety of thoughts ran through my mind regarding the real reason behind what I believed to be a mask propaganda campaign. During the pandemic while I was on one of my trips to the grocery store and before mask wearing was mandated, I felt like I was in the grocery store scene in

---

173. cielo.isciii.es, SciELO Espana, Scientific Electronic Library
Online, Preliminary report on surgical mask induced deoxygenation
during major surgery, http://scielo.isciii.es/pdf/neuro/v19n2/3.pdf.

the movie, *The Stepford Wives*, where all of the women are in lock step as far as how they look, act, speak, and behave. I was the only person I saw without a mask. I exited the store without buying a thing.

I believe there is a spiritual component to the mask—in the fight of good versus evil.

Author, film producer, speaker, and researcher Steve Quayle brought interesting points to light regarding the "masking" of the world. He spoke about the reasons for mask wearing in history.

> The mask in history was always meant to do two things. Primarily to hide a person's identity who is involved in some evil, or to get them on the stage or the theatre in a play, or presentation, with another persona. Most people never even consider this and I didn't until I was praying about it and the Lord gave me this … He said the devil hates my likeness and image and mankind … while he's destroying mankind, he also is hiding mankind and the image that I placed into each and every one of My children… .
>
> What's a smile worth? When you smile at someone there is an embrace—a hug—notice this, that the mask is covering up … the man, the image and likeness of God is absolutely being marred."[174]

This statement fits perfectly with what I said earlier; and this is the spiritual reason for the mask, although most people see only the physical implications.

For a society that is always touting they are not judgmental—shouting down or shaming someone for not wearing a mask was indeed judgmental. Another point to keep in mind is that we cannot know what health issues someone else has that could become escalated by wearing a mask—and frankly it is *none* of our business.

174. Steve Quayle - "The Mask and Mark of Zoros - Final Warning" - Full Show - 8/13/2020 YouTube.com https://www.youtube.com/watch?v=L7cuOcdxGuc.

## Pandemic Wrap Up

I could go on with more connections about what I think this pandemic was really about, but that would be another book. There is too much to cover. From the coincidental mock Event 201 that happened only weeks before the pandemic hit China, to the relationships between the Gates Foundation, Pirbright, and Fauci, and the money made by Big Pharma and Gates and everyone at the top. My goal was to reveal facts you may have not known regarding the pandemic.

I wanted to share the information I found and ask that you look at what I presented with a critical eye.

CHAPTER 8

# Technology, Technocracy, and Transhumanism

I believe we are on the cusp of a new era, where all societies on a global scale will be run by technology and technocrats in a technocratic tyranny. This goes hand in hand with the sustainable development agenda I discussed earlier in the environment chapter. It stems from the United Nations and funnels down to all nations worldwide. You may be asking, "What is a technocracy and what are technocrats?"

Executive Director of Citizens for Free Speech, author, and speaker Patrick Wood's book, *Technocracy Rising: The Trojan Horse of Global Transformation*, spells it out clearly, "Technocracy is transforming economics, government, religion, and law. It rules by regulation, not by Rule of Law, policies are dreamed up by unelected and unaccountable technocrats buried in government agencies, and regional governance structures are replacing sovereign entities like cities, counties, and states."[175]

The technocrats are those who rule under the technocracy. They can be from a variety of public or private organizations, self-proclaimed elitist individuals, politicians, nongovernmental organizations, corporations, and even local and state committees or groups. The key thing to remember

175. *Technocracy Rising: The Trojan Horse of Global Transformation*, Patrick M. Wood, Coherent Publishing, Mesa, AZ, preface, 2015.

is often they are "unelected"—the average person does not usually have a say in which of these people are appointed or put into which positions. In my opinion, the World Economic Forum is also part of the technocracy—Bill Gates, Klaus Schwab—people we did not elect; they are part of elite groups that come in issuing edicts, and yet not many people notice; they simply go along with their program.

I believe the leadership of all of the tech companies is part of this technocracy—the technocrats. In recent decades, Apple, Microsoft, PayPal, Google, YouTube, Facebook, Twitter, TikTok, and the like have had an amazingly huge amount of power and control in how we do business, what we buy, what we can post online, what we see posted online, online banking, how we find things online, surveillance, how we vote, who gets elected, who the trending celebrities are, what the trending news is, and so much more of our daily life.

In my opinion, these technocrats will use technology, probably in concert with governments, to try to rule with an iron fist primarily through information surveillance and control.

In a radio interview with Wood, he explained how technocracy is not a new idea and that there were technocrats in the 1920s and 1930s, but this movement might have started as early as the late 1800s. Technocracy is not a monetary-based supply and demand capitalist economic system that we are used to, but it is an economic system based on tracking and controlling energy consumption. When you look at this from the perspective of the United Nations' sustainable development agenda, it makes sense that technocrats will use energy consumption to gain and keep control of everyone and everything through energy usage. Wood explains,

> In the course of my research I ran across this historic movement from the 1930s.... I traveled to the University of Edmonton, up in Canada. I spent a week going through their archive col-

lection on technocracy ... the records, the letters, the pictures, the booklets, the magazines, you name it. It's just an amazing treasure trove ... any type of economic system, of course, would have to have a currency. It's like the lifeblood of the body. You have to have something that provides liquidity. And to the technocrats in those early days, they decided that energy would be the perfect source of currency in society, and therefore, they would do away with a national currency system, the Fiat paper system we have today ... and they would replace it with energy credits or energy currency.

The way they envisioned it back then was that at the beginning of a period like a month or a quarter, a forecast of the energy produced would be made and it would be divided by the population. And everybody would receive their allocation of energy credits or energy, and they could use those units to spend on goods and services that were priced according to the energy that went in to making them. So theoretically, if you went to buy a blouse, for instance, you could make some pretty detailed assumptions about, well, the cotton was raised in Egypt, and then it traveled on a boat to Sri Lanka and sewing machines sewed it up, and then it went on a boat again and went to Walmart or whatever. And you could kind of figure out how much energy went into make each thing in society that would be bought, and that's how things would be priced.

There would be no supply and demand. There would be no choices ... they would control all of the means of production and all the means of consumption. And that means that they would decide what needed to be made and then would have it made, and then it would be distributed to the population for consumption. One of the very devious and radical things about technocracy with the energy currency that I've just described is that they specified that they were wasting currency in the sense that at the end of the period, any leftover units not spent would just dissipate. They would just terminate, become worthless, and you would get a new allocation for the next period. So there was no ability to save money. They figured, what do you need to save money for anyway? All your needs are taken care of, and that means you couldn't leave any inheritance to your children.

...Basically you're just living month to month, and they would hand them (*credits*) out at the insistence of these engineers and scientists and technicians who felt like they and they alone were able to run the world.[176]

Wood also writes in his book that technocracy means replacement of government as we know it. He says that governance will be a process of regulatory management versus representative government. Unelected experts will be the regulators. If you pay attention, you can see this on a local level in municipalities around the country. It seems there are unelected members that sit on local boards and committees; they have substantial input and impact on government decisions, decision-makers, and policies.

In our interview Wood continued, "They're pushing this down into every local community around the country. And I mean *every* community. You can hardly go anywhere without seeing it … look at the county zoning commission, for instance, the county board of supervisors. You look at the city council, you look at the city managers, you look at the staff people creating some of the plans and stuff for the future. You'll find this technocracy mantra, this sustainable development mantra everywhere you look in America today. And the net is being drawn tighter and tighter."[177]

---

176. *Truth Seekers Radio Show*, Episode 60, Patrick Wood, author of *Technocracy Rising: The Trojan Horse of Global Transformation*, 2016.

177. Ibid.

According to Wood technocracy is the science of social engineering and the scientific operations of the entire social mechanism to produce and distribute goods and services to the entire population. This scientific operation does not include any sense of governance, only those who are appointed. The scientists and engineers are considered the only ones smart enough to put together a system to make society work—a scientific dictatorship.

The natural question would be, how would they keep control and police such a dictatorship? I believe this is where the surveillance society we see emerging in all areas of life comes in. As Wood pointed out, "Virtually everything we do is being harvested and stored within a central repository. And I mean everything—phone calls, emails, all your social media activity … all things are being monitored right now by our government … there's no such thing as too much data."[178]

## Monitoring the Technocracy

Wood describes the surveillance system for the technocracy, what is known as the Smart Grid. This is the wireless technology system that redesigns the power grid, giving the ability to monitor and control consumers' energy consumption via continuous two-way communications. The rollout began around 2012 and is still in progress today. The Smart Grid is based on technology called "Internet of Things" (IoT) defined on TechTarget.com as "…a system of interrelated computing devices, mechanical and digital machines, objects, animals or people that are provided with unique identifiers (UIDs) and the ability to transfer data over a network without requiring human-to-human or human-to-computer interaction … an IoT ecosystem consists of web-enabled smart devices that use embedded systems, such as processors, sensors and communica-

---

178. Ibid.

tion hardware, to collect, send and act on data they acquire from their environments."[179]

So if you are marked with a unique identifier, you can be tracked. Essentially, you are being tracked now through your smart devices. I believe this is only the beginning.

The best way I can explain it is to think of every person and every object acting as an individual antenna that makes up a network of antennae in a large web-based network. Any data that comes from the antennae is collected, stored, monitored, and surveilled 24 hours, 7 days a week everywhere worldwide.

Elana Freeland, teacher, researcher, and author of *Chemtrails, HAARP and the Full Spectrum Dominance of Planet Earth*, explained her research findings on the Internet of Things and developed the antenna idea in a radio interview in 2016. She told me that for decades governments have been bathing us and all nature's living things in heavy metals that are highly conductive. Chemicals are sprayed in our air, water, and food.

Freeland states that in order to activate this system, they need all living things to be doused in a backdrop of heavy metals to be picked up on what I call the radar.

> We live in a nano-particulate world of science and there are various systems. Our water, our GMO foods, our sky … you realize that there is a vast experiment going on through the delivery system that can enter our lungs and from there our blood system and from there the tissues of our entire body… and they can deliver any number of things— if it's on a nanoscale … I am saying that on a nanoscale, the chemtrails that are being laid over our heads have many things in them. Some of them are heavy metals, which are highly conductive,

---

179. TechTarget.com, What is the internet of things (IoT)?, by Alexander S. Gillis, https://www.techtarget.com/iotagenda/definition/Internet-of-Things-IoT.

and that would be aluminum, barium, strontium, titanium, and sometimes lithium.[180]

Freeland continues her findings on surveillance,

> With all the towers and the cell phones, all the electronics that we have now been given by the military, and I might remind you, the military had all this a generation before we did: computers, cell phones, televisions, you name it. We now are wired, and we are plugged in to this battery ready antenna-like atmosphere so the surveillance that can go on now is not just on your phone ... I'm talking about a surveillance that goes all the way to the sensors and the microprocessors in your bloodstream. They can follow everything from space, from land, it doesn't really matter because they have the computer power. All of this is one package that spells a fascist control over all life on Earth.[181]

She even sums up our conversation, saying that she believes the surveillance society will eventually lead to monitoring your thoughts because even thoughts have a frequency that they can tune in to.

If you think Freeland's ideas and research sound too outlandish, welcome to Elon Musk's Neuralink. This is exactly what the billionaire entrepreneur and influencer planned to develop when he first announced the project in 2017.

Musk announced a project that would design brain-computer interface technology, and an article published by Gizmodo states: "Neuralink will attempt to use 'ultra-high bandwidth brain-machine interfaces to connect humans and computers,' or more simply, to connect human brains with

---

180. Truth Seekers Radio Show, Episode 49, Elana Freeland, author of Chemtrails, HAARP, and the Full Spectrum Dominance of Planet Earth, 2016.
181. Ibid.

computers via implantable brain chips."[182]

If they are connecting the human brain to a computer interface, is it so far off to think they could eventually monitor thoughts, or even create or manipulate them? Of course the article discusses the humanitarian uses, such as treating disease or mental issues such as depression, while it ignores the possibility of future brain technology monitoring or surveilling thought.

While trying to find the current status of the Neuralink project, I came across a *Business Insider* article that discussed a possible conflict of interest related to Musk's business practices and "testing its brain implants on animals ahead of plans for human trials." Apparently, there were people that were up in arms over Musk's animal testing activities.

But what I thought was more newsworthy was a statement regarding computer capability to translate a person's thoughts.[183] To translate thoughts, you would first be required to read those thoughts. I believe this is the linchpin to a future total surveillance society.

In my opinion, this substantiates Freeland's statement about thought surveillance, and shows that this is highly likely and not so farfetched after all.

## Transhumanism: the Final Frontier

All of the pieces of information I've discussed so far in this chapter, in my opinion, are stepping stones to bring us to what this spiritual battle is about, from a technocratic society to the Internet of Things network, thought surveillance technology, and finally what I call the final frontier, Transhumanism.

---

182. Gizmodo.com, What to Know About Neuralink, Elon Musk's Brain-Computer Interface Project, Aug. 24, 2020, by George Dvorsky, https://gizmodo.com/what-to-know-about-neuralink-elon-musk-s-brain-compute-1844751895.

183. *Business Insider*, "Elon Musk's Neuralink accused of 'obvious conflict of interest' by filling its animal-testing regulatory committee with staff who could profit, report says." May 5, 2023, by Pete Syme, https://www.msn.com/en-us/news/technology/elon-musks-neuralink-accused-of-obvious-conflict-of-interest-by-filling-its-animal-testing-regulatory-committee-with-staff-who-could-profit-report-says/ar-AA1aMvlq.

As I mentioned earlier, I believe Transhumanism is an updated form of the eugenics movement, but on steroids—the melding of humans with machines to pervert the man God made in His image.

While the eugenics movement was about ridding society of what the elites believed were undesirable humans, the transhumanism movement longs to create a super race by enhancing humans through crossing them with technology.

Transhumanism is a philosophical and social movement that advocates the use of science and technology to enhance human physical, cognitive, and emotional abilities beyond what humans' natural capabilities would normally be—through the merging of humans with technology.[184]

Thought leaders in this area believe that through the use of advanced technologies such as genetic engineering, artificial intelligence, and biotechnology, humans can transcend their biological limitations and achieve a higher level of existence, and in some cases even have eternal life.[185]

While the transhumanist movement would like to sell their philosophy by saying it can help solve the world's problems, I believe what they don't tell us is that altering man into a hybrid may also edit a man's soul and that can lead to his spiritual destruction from which there is no turning back. This is the same game that was played in the garden of Eden in the book of Genesis chapter 3 verse 4: "And the serpent said unto the woman, 'Ye shall not surely die.'"

To reach their transhumanistic utopian society, they first have to promote the destruction of man—a post human society, posthumanism, a future state of existence without humans, or as a Wikipedia entry puts it, "after humans"[186]—in my opinion this means without humans.

184. Wikipedia.com, Transhumanism, https://en.wikipedia.org/wiki/Transhumanism.

185. Newsweek.com, AI and Transhumanism: Could Quest for Super-intelligence and Eternal Life Lead to a Dystopian Nightmare?, Alexander Thomas, August 2017, https://www.newsweek.com/ai-transhumanism-super-intelligence-dystopian-nightmare-644128.

186. Wikipedia.com, Posthumanism, https://en.wikipedia.org/wiki/Posthumanism.

These would be individuals who have undergone significant technological changes, including: genetic engineering, brain-computer interfaces (such as the Neuralink tech), or nanotechnology that will supposedly bring them to a higher level of consciousness without physical limitations, and eternal life.

I have questions regarding the moral consequences of modifying what was made by almighty God.

What is the endgame of these enhancements? If we start to alter DNA, what will be the state of the subhuman race? And most importantly, is all of this so-called technological science enhancement ideology about helping humans, or is it about Satan perverting what God created? If these beings are modified, and their offspring are so genetically far from humans, could they be born without a soul?

In his book, *Mass Awakening*, Paul McGuire says that the human race is at a final turning point. "The science of Transhumanism is creating a race of super humans through creating and changing DNA ... a new race of humans which are a combination of genetic engineering, new DNA, and robotic, Android, and computer technologies. Thus man is now being reinvented as an integration of man and machine... . If one believes in a God, the question arises, 'Do these new humans and clones have souls?'"[187]

In Christianity, Jesus Christ was sent to save man from sin through His death, burial, and resurrection. Could the spiritual endgame be that Satan is trying to undo what Christ did on earth? Could it be that subhumans would not be covered under the blood of the Lamb, Jesus Christ? Is this why they are working to replace man, humans, with their copies, transhumans?

The scientists, bioengineers, technocrats, and other elites funding these

---

187. Paul McGuire, *Mass Awakening*, (M House Publishers, Los Angeles, CA, 2015), p. 219.

projects aren't talking about these concerns. Is it because they know the answers and may be hiding the truth?

Even if you are not concerned with the spiritual aspect of this, what are some of the unintended consequences in the physical realm, such as loss of autonomy, identity, and human connection? Do we want to turn all people into unfeeling, stoic robots that have no individual identity and no freedom, or worse yet, no yearning to be free—a willing slave class only created for one purpose, to serve the elites?

Transhumanism is gaining public notice more every day. As it gains more mainstream attention and people start to wrap their brains around what it means, the propaganda machine is already gearing up to demonize those who are not in lock-step with their plan. Ordained priest in the Church of Sweden, professor of systematic theology, and writer Stefan Lindholm reveals this in an article he wrote regarding transhumanism:

"And what's a revolutionary movement without reactionaries? Anyone who resists this pendulum swing will be branded 'bio-conservative' or even 'bio-Luddite' by the transhumanists, who argue that leaving "old" biology behind will not be a great loss, because we are not limited to our biological and evolutionary origins by any kind of determinism—divine or materialistic."[188]

In other words, according to them, the almighty God did not know what He was doing, and they can do it better. History has proven them wrong. All you have to do is look at the state of every area of society in the world today—there's nothing new under the sun.

Ecclesiastes 1:9 tells us, "The thing that hath been, it is that which shall be; and that which is done is that which shall be done: and there is no new thing under the sun."

---

188. Acton Institute, Jacques Ellul and the Idols of Transhumanism (a book so italics?), by Stefan Lindholm, November 14, 2022, https://www.acton.org/religion-liberty/volume-35-number-4/ jacques-ellul-and-idols-transhumanism.

# CHAPTER 9

# China: Takeover and Death of a Nation

## U.S. Brings Communism to China

As I've mentioned many times during radio interviews and in this book, I went to grade school in Florida. The state was not known at the time for their great education system. When students transferred from other states, it seemed they were well ahead of what we were being taught. Needless to say, I never had much world history and certainly never heard about the U.S. and how it played a part in bringing China into communism.

When reading Dr. Stan Monteith's *Brotherhood of Darkness*, I was shocked when he wrote that the United States helped push China into communism. In hindsight, it is ironic that the Chinese communism we helped create—is the very sinister power that is now quietly seeping into our country and will likely take over if people don't wake up and stop it.

Dr. Monteith explained how the Truman administration helped usher in the communist takeover of China.

> I want to explain how Harry Truman brought communism
> to China. Most people believe that the Nationalist Chinese
> lost the civil war, but nothing could be further from the truth.
> General Chiang Kai-shek's armies were winning the civil war
> until the American State Department placed an embargo on the

Nationalist forces which prevented them from buying weapons or supplies anywhere in the world.... . How can an army fight without weapons? It can't. Contrary to everything you heard or read, our State Department intentionally brought Chairman Mao to power. To verify that charge, I quote from a long-suppressed Senate report on the fall of China.[189]

Monteith quotes from the Institute of Pacific Relations Report of the Committee on the Judiciary Eighty-Second Congress document:

At the end of 1945 when General Marshall left for China, the balance of power was with the Chinese Nationalists ... and remained so until at least June 1946 ... Chiang's divisions were chasing the Communists northward and the prospect of victory by Nationalist China was at its highest ... However, when General Marshall arrived in China, he undertook to bring about the coalition government which his directive demanded ... this plan failed when the coalition failed.

When the Chinese government did not effect the coalition, by the summer of 1946 United States military assistance to China was brought to an end. Not only did the United States stop sending military supplies to the Chinese Government; the shipment of war materials actually purchased by the Chinese also was halted.... . When the flow of American ammunition was stopped, these divisions lost their fire power and were defeated. Even after the Eightieth Congress appropriated $125,000,000 for aid to the Chinese, shipments were delayed and when the guns finally reached the Chinese general in north China, they were without bolts and therefore useless.[190]

---

189. Dr. Stanley Monteith, *Brotherhood of Darkness* (Oklahoma City, Hearthstone Publishing, 2000), p. 19-20.

190. Institute of Pacific Relations: Report of the Committee of the Judiciary, 82nd Congress, S. Res. 366, p. 204-205.

Monteith asks the obvious questions. Why would the State Department send the Nationalist Chinese guns without bolts? He surmises that it is impossible to come to another conclusion after reading the McCarren Committee Report. The Truman administration purposely set the Nationalist Chinese up for the failure that led to Chairman Mao's rise to power.

In his book and on his radio program, *Radio Liberty*, Dr. Monteith often talked about what he called "the great foundations." He explained how these tax-exempt entities helped carry out insidious tasks that were part of the elites' overall plan. They were responsible for funding communist activities, disseminating propaganda, and supporting organized civil groups, politicians, business leaders, and various other institutions to help put parts of their plan in motion.

Dr. Monteith reveals some of these great foundations that help fund propaganda and in turn lead to activities that propagate a particular agenda.

The Senate appointed a special committee to investigate why the State Department placed an arms embargo on the Nationalist Chinese that led to their failure. During the investigation, they discovered the Rockefeller and Ford Foundations had been funding Chinese outlets with communist propaganda, years before China fell to communism.

The 83rd Congress commissioned Congressman B. Carroll Reece to investigate the tax-exempt foundations to determine why they had financed communist organizations. The Reece Committee discovered:

… In 1915 the Carnegie Endowment for International Peace launched a propaganda program to force the United States into World War I.

… Many of our large foundations were actively promoting communism and socialism… .

The Rockefeller Foundation, the Carnegie Educational Foundation, and the Ford Foundation had used their grant-making power to take over American education and force colleges and universities to abandon their religious beliefs and moral standards…

Foundations influenced State Department policy and were largely responsible for bringing communism to China.[191]

Why would the great foundations do this? What is their end game? Again, this is just a small cog in the wheel of the overall operation that has been underway for decades to bring American society to its knees. Once this happens, after a short time, the New World Order will be put in place. No freedom will lead to disorder, and this creates the environment needed to bring forth their World Order.

An article in *The American Conservative* gives insight into a historical example of why the great foundations were created and how they have increased their political and social influence within American institutions.

Ford Foundation was founded in the 30s by auto king Henry Ford and his son Edsel as a way to shield the Ford Motor company's profits from confiscatory taxes. The organization embraced a "socially conscious" grantmaking role in the 60s. Heather MacDonald of the Manhattan Institute writes that the charity 'sparked the key revolution in the foundation world-view: the idea that foundations were to improve the lot of mankind not by building lasting institutions but by challenging existing ones' … the Ford Foundation is helping the Chinese

---

191. Dr. Stanley Monteith, *Brotherhood of Darkness* (Oklahoma City, Hearthstone Publishing, 2000), p. 52-53.

government make money and enhance its reputation at home and abroad.[192]

Reputation is the most important reason in my opinion. They need to re-brand communism to get wider acceptance of it. They have to re-tool how Americans view communist China, especially older generations of Americans who learned how communism means living without liberty and freedom. As they die off and the younger generations accept the new, kinder, gentler communism that the great foundations have helped redefine, younger people will accept communism with open arms. They will willingly walk into their own enslavement.

To give you a more recent example of the great foundations being instrumental in the chaos we are experiencing today, another article published in *The American Conservative* reports how the Ford Foundation is in bed with the Chinese Communist Party (CCP) and their role is funding the efforts for the great Chinese takeover of America. Reporter James Lynch, explains:

> In September of last year, The American Conservative shone a spotlight on the Ford Foundation's deep ties to the Chinese Communist Party. Since 1979, the massive foundation has been one of the only foreign charities allowed in China, and that previous feature demonstrated how Ford is actively assisting the Chinese government in exporting their communist values elsewhere.... Thorough examination of public disclosures suggests that Ford's funding of Chinese operations goes far beyond economic development and foreign influence. According to the foundation's website, Ford has given $41.8 million to education projects in China over the past 15 years. Buried in a report

---

192. TheAmericanConservative.com, How The Ford Foundation Became An Instrument Of Chinese Foreign Policy, by Sloan Rachmuth, Sept. 22, 2020, https://www.theamericanconservative.com/articles/how-the-ford-foundation-is-helping-support-chinese-foreign-policy/.

reviewing the Ford Foundation's grant making in education and culture in China from 2001 to 2016 is a disclosure that the foundation provided grants to an educational entity known as the Horizon Education Center of China to fund education reform in Xinjiang.[193]

Why would the Ford Foundation pour so much money into Chinese educational institutions? Do you think they support teaching freedom and capitalist ideas in a communist-led country?

The Great Foundations were originally created to be a tax shield vehicle for the companies that spawned them. It seems they have since moved into helping push foreign and domestic policies and agendas that have a definite socialist, communist nature.

Lynch continues:

> Dating back to 2009, Horizon has been working on a vocational education reform program in Xinjiang. According to a BBC report, talk of "vocational education and training" programs in Xinjiang is Chinese Communist Party propaganda for the re-education camps for Uyghur Muslims, which are alleged to be full of human rights abuses…. Another educational initiative funded by the Ford Foundation was the "100,000 strong" campaign promoted during the Obama administration by former Secretary of State Hillary Clinton, who strongly backed the 2012 effort to get 100,000 American students studying in China by 2014. The goal of the initiative was "fostering people-to-people exchange and understanding between the United States and China."[194]

I first discovered the Chinese education exchange programs that had

---

193. TheAmericanConservative.com, The Ford Foundation Is Funding CCP Propaganda, by James Lynch, March 22, 2021, https://www.theamericanconservative.com/articles/the-ford-foundation-is-funding-ccp-propaganda/.

194. Ibid.

already infiltrated the U.S. university system, while doing research on information that pointed to plans that brought wholly Chinese-owned economic zones into U.S. cities across the country.

## Slow Education Infiltration?

While doing research about Chinese investment in Toledo, I found myself down another rabbit hole when I visited the University of Toledo website and found a release published in 2013, but noted that since 2008 a Chinese delegation from the Zheijang University of Finance and Economics had been making trips to the university to learn about business management. The release went on to say that this year would be different and they wanted to focus on higher education management.

My question is: Who is learning from whom? Do the Chinese really want to learn from our universities, or are our universities being infiltrated?

Here is a snippet from the release; notice the name of the director of the UT Confucius Institute, Dr. Aige Guo, who coordinated the visit. Yes, the University of Toledo has a UT Confucius Institute—nothing to worry about here, right?

"The model we are creating for this delegation visit is one we hope can be replicated with other delegation visits to UT in the future," said Dr. Ron Opp, UT associate professor of educational leadership and the doctoral program coordinator in higher education, who is coordinating the educational component.

Dr. Aige Guo, the director of the UT Confucius Institute, is coordinating the logistics for this visit."[195]

When I did a search to learn the mission of the UT Confucius Institute,

---

195. University of Toledo, Chinese delegation to visit UT to learn about U.S. education management, July 11, 2013, News, UToday, Education, Health Science and Human Service, by Samantha Watson, http://news.utoledo.edu/index.php/07_11_2013/chinese-delegation-to-visit-ut-to-learn-about-u-s-education-management.

I found that these institutes are in universities across the country. Some schools include The University of Buffalo and the University of Utah, as well as colleges in Atlanta, Charlotte, Orlando, Huntsville, Nashville, and Memphis, to name a few cities.

The mission for the Confucius Institute on the University of Toledo website says, "Confucius Institute at The University of Toledo is committed to serving the region of Northwest Ohio by providing education in Chinese language and culture, developing and enhancing China-related scholarly research/discovery, academic programs, and educational and training programs that support business outreach and engagement, and offering opportunities for cultural exchanges between China and the United States of America."[196]

This all sounds warm and fuzzy.

*The American Conservative* article expands on the true nature of the Confucius Institute in American universities. "As thousands of American dollars go towards universities teaching Chinese propaganda, the CCP has continued making its presence known with Confucius Institutes in universities across the United States. On top of that, the Chinese Communist Party has begun using the woke ideology supported by Black Lives Matter and many American universities to further its global ambitions."[197]

My research revealed that in 2008 the Chinese delegation started to make trips to the U.S. university, Bush was still in office. The article was published five years later during the Obama administration. Although I believe the Obama administration was pivotal in helping China gain a foothold in U.S. institutions during his watch, I think he picked up where the Clinton and Bush administrations left off.

196. The University of Toledo, Confucius Institute at the University of Toledo, https://www.utoledo.edu/cisp/Confucius_Institute/.

197. TheAmericanConservative.com, The Ford Foundation Is Funding CCP Propaganda, by James Lynch, March 22, 2021, https://www.theamericanconservative.com/articles/the-ford-foundation-is-funding-ccp-propaganda/.

I am not saying that learning other languages or learning about other cultures is a bad thing, but I believe this has nothing to do with that and instead may be one of many steps in China's strategy to reach their major goal—a takeover of the United States.

## Chinese Control in U.S. Cities?

When I did a report in 2013 on planned Chinese-owned zones in U.S. cities, I stumbled on a story about how we (the U.S. government) were sending to China U.S. politicians of all levels from national to local. Back then it seemed strange that we would be doing this, and I suspected there was more to it.

This is when I first learned that Chinese nationals were being encouraged to come to the U.S. to buy land in different areas that could potentially be controlled by the Chinese government. How could an international communist government have jurisdiction over these Chinese communities and lands located in the middle of our country?

## Boise and Chinese Investment

The first report I heard about was in the Boise, Idaho, area. It was a 50 square mile by 50 square mile area that would be built around a manufacturing plant that was potentially going to be a Chinese territory under the Chinese government due to a loophole—the manufacturing company that wanted to buy the real estate for the plant was majority owned by the Communist Chinese Party. I looked into this claim further and found this statement in the *Idaho Statesman*:

> A Chinese national company is interested in developing a
> 10,000 to 30,000-acre technology zone for industry, retail
> centers and homes south of the Boise Airport. Officials of the
> China National Machinery Industry Corp. have broached the

idea—based on a concept popular in China today—to city and state leaders. They are also interested in helping build and finance a fertilizer plant near American Falls, an idea company officials returned to Idaho this month to pursue. This ambitious, long-term proposal would start with a manufacturing and warehouse zone tied to the airport, and could signify a shift in the economic relationship between the two superpowers. [198]

Since this article had been published in 2011, I tried to find follow-up stories on the Boise plans to see what happened with the Chinese project, but I found none. I decided to contact the *Idaho Statesman* reporter to see if he could offer insight.

He basically said the project never got off the ground because the story stirred up concern about the Chinese company's plans. This resulted in a nationwide protest that caused the company to lose interest, and they decided not to go forward with the plan.

This is a perfect example showing that if people would step up and make their beliefs and policy concerns known, they could make a difference—not only locally, but they might even ignite a fire that could make an impact nationwide.

## Catskills and Chinese Investment

Another project I heard about was an aggressive project proposed by a Chinese developer who wanted to build "A China City" theme park in the Catskills in upstate New York.

According to a story published in 2013 by *The Sullivan County Democrat*, here is what the proposed plan included:

"A thousand homes. Fifty-six "ethnic villages." Two hundred fifty hotel rooms. Nearly 5 million square feet of commercial space. And a year-

---

198. Idaho Statesman, Chinese company eyes Boise, by Rocky Barker, June 2011, https://www.idahostatesman.com/news/local/community/boise/article40719738.html.

round amusement park. That's the $6 billion plan for more than 2,000 acres spanning Route 17 between Rock Hill and Wurtsboro Hills…. 'We already have the land under contract,' China City of America Chairman and CEO Sherry Li told a packed Thompson Town Hall that evening …"199

The article expands on how the Chinese investment is based on an immigration program:

"…the plan is predicated on outside investment—Chinese, in particular—through a federal immigration program. Known as "EB-5," the program encourages foreign investment on U.S. soil by promising visas (green cards) to immigrants who invest at least $500,000 in an American-based project ($1 million in urban and suburban areas)…Li's plan is to offer such opportunities to Chinese families interested in having their children attend the complex's private school and then an American university. She said she's in the final stages of gaining federal approval to do so."200

I tried to learn the status of the Catskills project because I never heard much more about it.

In 2018, the *Epoch Times* did a follow-up report on the original story. It stated the project that was proposed as a very grandiose development plan had been scaled down pretty much to the educational piece of the project.

> In an upstate New York town of roughly 15,000, a Long Island developer is facing pushback for plans to build a Chinese education center using the controversial EB-5 investor program that trades foreign investment for United States citizenship.
>
> The Thompson Education Center (TEC), which is predominantly in the town of Thompson with a portion in the town of

199. The Sullivan County Democrat, Chinese City, By Dan Hust, May 2013, http://www.sc-democrat.com/news/2013May/17/news.htm.

200. The Sullivan County Democrat, Chinese City, By Dan Hust, May 2013, http://www.sc-democrat.com/news/2013May/17/news.htm.

Fallsburg, was first proposed in 2013 as China City of America, a "Chinese Disneyland" with an amusement park, an education center, a hotel, housing, and a mall.

Over time, the project was whittled down to just the education center with some on-campus housing, a hotel, a museum, a library, and other education-related buildings.

The various incarnations of the project have received a warm welcome by local development and tourism organizations, but it's also facing opposition from locals who see it as out of place in their bucolic community, and a threat to the environment and their way of life.[201]

The China City of America's own Wikipedia page states the following about the status of the project, "While the larger China City project has stalled, the Thompson Education Center (TEC) is still being planned. The proposed for-profit college campus is on a 573-acre parcel of land near Route 17, Exit 112, which borders Wild Turnpike in Thompson, New York, and extends to the town of Mamakating."[202]

As a side note about the visa program being used to attract Chinese investment, the EB-5 federal visa program "provides a method for eligible Immigrant Investors to become lawful permanent residents ... by investing substantial capital to finance a business in the United States that will employ at least 10 American workers."[203]

This seems like a pretty good trade-off for those who can afford to take part in this program. You pay to play in a business investment that stands to make a return for you, and you get U.S. citizenship as a big bonus! Apparently the current amount to invest is a minimum of $500,000.

201. TheEpochTimes.com, Controversial Chinese College Project Being Built Upstate NY Faces Obstacles, May 2018, Holly Kellum, https://www.theepochtimes.com/controversial-chinese-college-project-being-built-upstate-ny-faces-obstacles_2295851.html.

202. Wikipedia, China City of America, https://en.wikipedia.org/wiki/China_City_of_America.

203. Wikipedia, EB-5 visa, https://en.wikipedia.org/wiki/EB-5_visa.

## Toledo and Chinese Investment

Toledo was once known for manufacturing glass and auto parts. Between 2000 and 2014, they suffered 140 factory closings. A report by *The Guardian* explained how Toledo Mayor, Michael Bell, decided he probably would not get much help from Washington D.C., so he tried another tactic to bring economic revitalization to the area.

"Knowing he was unlikely to get much help from Washington in attracting investment, he decided he'd go drum it up himself. He made China his city's top foreign target for investment and led several trade trips to China personally."[204]

His trips seemed to have paid off. According to a 2014 announcement by The Midwest USA Chinese Chamber of Commerce (which I never knew existed), it was worth the work. "During his term he courted hundreds of Chinese investors, which so far has amounted in more than $10 million in investment."[205]

As I stated earlier, I noticed a number of American politicians of all levels, especially at state and local levels, making trips to China. This article titled, "An American Waterfront (Made in China)," pulled back the curtain on why.

"Every mayor, every governor is traipsing off to China, but it's a middle person that is trusted on both sides that can make things happen quicker ... Toledo is hardly alone among American cities in wanting to attract some of what Chinese citizens are investing abroad ... just a week earlier, U.S.-China Investment Week events were held in Milwaukee, Orlando, Washington, D.C., Portland, Los Angeles, and Dallas. Texas

---

204. TheGuardian.com, Toledo goes to China: can small cities go it alone on the global stage?, May 15, 2014, Aaron M. Renn, https://www.theguardian.com/cities/2014/may/15/toledo-china-small-cities -global-stage.

205. Midwest USA Chinese Chamber of Commerce, LUNAR NEW YEAR GALA: MAYOR MICHAEL BELL TO SHARE CHINESE STORY, Posted on January 15, 2014, https://www.china-midwest. com/2014/01/15/gala-speaker/.

Gov. Rick Perry attended the gathering at Cowboys Stadium; the dinner gala guest of honor was George W. Bush."[206]

This article highlights an event in Toledo that was organized by a group called the Five Lakes Global Economic Forum. They invited 150 Chinese investors to the area to wine and dine them while getting them to *explore investing* in the area. Some of the Toledo sites purchased by Chinese investors included:

" ... the spring 2011 sale of two sites along the east side of the Maumee River that runs through Toledo.

The Docks, a strip of destination restaurants developed in the 1990s, went for $2.5 million, and a 69-acre parcel in the Marina District went for $3.8 million ... the two sites had been for sale for a while, with no takers until Dashing Pacific Group Ltd., made up of Yuan Xiaohong and Wu Kin Hung. Later came the sale of the Park Inn itself to an undisclosed Chinese investor for a bargain $3 million."[207]

All of this said, I still believe that we as a country have to be guarded on foreign investment deals in the U.S. We can't be naive and let a foreign entity with money come in and buy, thinking there will be no consequences down the line.

In my opinion, most of our politicians and government servants are for sale and do not care whom they sell to, as long as the cash is there.

So why should we care?

When most of the country becomes foreign-owned, we are no longer the U.S. but become the property of the foreign owners, their culture, ethics, and in my opinion, eventually their laws.

As an example, on a side note about culture, I learned about a Chinese

206. NextCity.org, An American Waterfront (Made In China), Nancy Scola, Oct. 29, 2012, https://nextcity.org/features/view/An-American-waterfront-made-in-china.

207. NextCity.org, An American Waterfront (Made In China), Nancy Scola, Oct. 29, 2012, https://nextcity.org/features/view/An-American-waterfront-made-in-china.

glass company that opened a U.S. manufacturing plant in another Ohio city under former presidential candidate and governor John Kasich, as announced by the *Dayton Daily News:*

> Ohio Gov. John Kasich and Fuyao Chairman and founder Cao Dewang will make an announcement today in Columbus about Fuyao Glass America Inc., according to Kasich's office … It is expected to invest $250 million in the plant, transforming it into country's biggest plants for finishing automotive glass. Fuyao will take raw glass and heat, shape, and fit it in Moraine for use in autos. Landing the Fuyao project was one of the biggest coups of JobsOhio and the Kasich administration. The deal was inked 12 months ago and in May the Ohio Tax Credit Authority voted to give a 15-year tax credit worth up to nearly $10 million to Fuyao.[208]

Apparently, after the glass manufacturing company was up and running, a documentary film that was released showed how Chinese culture in terms of business does not put up with workers who want to be treated fairly.

"Chinese-owned Fuyao Glass America Inc. is facing blowback from a Netflix documentary showing the company's chairman and managers making disparaging comments about American workers and their attempts to form a union at the Moraine, Ohio, plant."[209]

This Chinese manager did not seem to hide his cultural beliefs regarding where American worker norms and rights stand in his organization.

"In the documentary, Mr. Cao says, 'If a union comes in, I am shutting

---

208. Dayton Daily News, Governor, CEO to make Fuyao announcement today, by Laura A. Bischoff, Jan. 13, 2015, https://www.daytondailynews.com/business/governor-ceo-make-fuyao-announcement-today/vJODMKDBQCXEVIWB3AygfI/.

209. Bloomberg Law, Obama-Backed Netflix Documentary Causes Headaches for Fuyao Glass, August 30, 2019, Hassan A. Kanu and Alex Ebert, https://news.bloomberglaw.com/daily-labor-report/obama-backed-netflix-documentary-causes-headaches-for-fuyao-glass.

down,' during a management meeting in one scene. In another, a manager shows an employee's picture to the camera, describes the man as a friend and union supporter, then says, 'He'll be fired in short order.' The documentary also shows the unsafe working conditions of the workers—some of them are collecting broken glass with bare hands, and others are forced to engage in much more dangerous tasks."[210]

Americans, in general, have believed in fairness and worker's rights. Chinese culture is different. American workers need to understand this. According to an article published in *Bloomberg Law*, Charlotte Garden, a labor and employment and Constitutional law professor, stated that some of the management statements and actions seen in the film are violations of the National Labor Relations Act.[211]

That may be so in our culture, but do you think these Chinese businessmen really care about that?

In my opinion, Chinese investment will stop if they have to put up with the way our labor culture has traditionally been regulated and conducted.

And what do you think our political prostitutes will do when Chinese investors threaten to stop investment money in the U.S.? Will they stand firm by American workers' rights? Don't hold your breath. I think they will simply sell out. I would not be surprised if Chinese companies that come here under investment terms will be able to eventually broker deals where their foreign investment will be predicated on a wavier of U.S. labor laws, with the ability to operate under Chinese law on U.S. soil.

210. EqualOcean.com, Manufacturing Glass for the Automobile Industry: Fuyao Group, May 27, 2020, by Bozde Celik, https://equalocean.com/analysis/2020052714035.

211. Bloomberg Law, Obama-Backed Netflix Documentary Causes Headaches for Fuyao Glass, August 30, 2019, Hassan A. Kanu & Alex Ebert, https://news.bloomberglaw.com/daily-labor-report/obama-backed-netflix-documentary-causes-headaches-for-fuyao-glass.

## Chinese Involvement in U.S. Telecommunications

The Chinese don't just have a foothold in business; apparently they've also had a stranglehold in U.S. telecommunications.

A bipartisan Senate report called, Threats to U.S. Networks: Oversight of Chinese Government-Owned Carriers, released in June 2020, describes a discovery made by a government subcommittee investigation led by Senator Rob Portman (R-OH) and Senator Tom Carper (D-DE) that revealed little to no oversight of Chinese state-owned telecommunications carriers that have been operating in the United States for the last two decades.

The government report revealed national security concerns in terms of Chinese espionage efforts.

The report states, " … U.S. government officials have warned that Chinese state-owned carriers are "subject to exploitation, influence, and control by the Chinese government" and can be used in the Chinese government's cyber and economic espionage efforts targeted at the United States… ."[212]

That's a shocker! While we give them the gateway, they use their own Chinese telecomms to spy on us from within the U.S.

How did this happen in the United States? Again, I say U.S. politicians are getting paid to look the other way. It is my belief they are for sale! The answer to the question, "How did this happen?" is divulged in the report:

"Currently, Chinese state-owned carriers are providing international telecommunications services based on Federal Communication Commission (FCC) authorizations granted more than a decade ago, in some cases nearly two decades. The carriers have provided services during

---

212. U.S. Senate Committee on Homeland Security & Governmental Affairs, Portman, Carper: Threats to U.S. Networks: Oversight of Chinese Government Owned Carriers, June 9, 2020, https://www.hsgac.senate.gov/wp-content/uploads/imo/media/doc/2020-06-09%20PSI%20Staff%20Report%20-%20Threats%20to%20U.S.%20Communications%20Networks.pdf, p. 23.

this time, with minimal oversight from Team Telecom."[213]

The report defines *Team Telecom* as "...three agencies—Department of Justice (DOJ), Department of Homeland Security (DHS), and the Department of Defense ("DOD"), which until recently were collectively referred to as "Team Telecom"....tasked with evaluating national security and law enforcement concerns."[214]

While the FCC has given its blessing to Chinese-owned telecomms to operate in the U.S., China has *not* provided equal access to U.S. telecomm companies.

"China does not provide U.S. telecommunications companies reciprocal access to the Chinese market and requires foreign carriers seeking to operate in China to enter into joint ventures with Chinese companies."[215]

Why do you think that is? Maybe it is so the Chinese government and their companies can keep an eye on U.S. company behaviors within their country. Isn't this what most sovereign countries would do to keep control of national security? Then why don't we do this? Disgusting! When did our country become so weak?

It is so plain to me why all of these U.S. government entities look the other way. Our country has been bought off, and now the new owners are slowly coming in and taking over, and the American people are oblivious to it.

To be fair, a government release was published by Homeland Security & Governmental Affairs in October 2021. It announced a move by the FCC to revoke a Chinese carrier's authorization as a follow-up to the original report.

The release states:

---

213. Ibid., p. 10.
214. Ibid., p. 3.
215. Ibid., p. 12.

Today's decision marks the first time the FCC has revoked a carrier's authorization to provide services based on national security concerns… 'As detailed in our bipartisan Permanent Subcommittee on Investigations report last year, China regularly uses its telecommunications carriers, including China Telecom Americas, to further its intelligence collection and espionage efforts,' said Senator Portman. 'I am pleased to see the FCC use its enforcement authority to address the threat to our national and economic security posed by China Telecom and ensure our communications networks are secure for all Americans. I urge the FCC to complete its review of the other Chinese-owned telecommunications carriers operating in the United States.'[216]

However, this only addressed China Telecom Americas; there are still other Chinese telecomm companies operating in the United States. Senator Carper's statement in this last release does not exactly give me confidence that the FCC will fix anything going forward. Their past actions are disgraceful at best.

Carper added, "I hope the FCC will continue its due diligence over other foreign-owned carriers operating in the U.S. to protect our domestic telecommunications networks going forward." [217]

## Chinese Involvement in U.S. Oil and Gas

So far I've discussed Chinese Communist Party infiltration in U.S. education, real estate, manufacturing, and telecomm—so oil and gas is not to be left out.

A *CNN Business* news story from October 2015 published a short news

---

216. Homeland Security & Governmental Affairs, Portman, Carper applaud FCC decision to end China Telecom operations in U.S., Oct. 26, 2021, https://www.hsgac.senate.gov/media/reps/portman-carper-applaud-fcc-decision-to-end-china-telecom-operations-in-us/.
217. Ibid.

brief that reported a Chinese investment holding company was set to buy Texas oil fields through a limited liability partnership for $1.3 billion.

And of course, the transaction had been approved by the U.S. Committee on Foreign Investment.[218] Then in May 2020, *Fox Business News* reported Texas energy companies were struggling and fighting risk of bankruptcy due to Covid shutdowns and might now result in foreign buyouts by Chinese investors—leaving control of more oil-producing land to foreign entities.

Finally, a voice of reason from Wayne Christian, commissioner of the Texas Railroad Commission that regulates the Texas oil and gas industry, "I believe it's a national security concern to allow unfriendly foreign countries to come in and buy land and oil in Texas and the United States … the federal government should watch very carefully and raise their standards on who can buy."[219]

To be fair, I was trying to get an update on any Chinese investment deals in Texas since Covid had created the struggling oil and gas environment. All of the stories seemed dated; however, there was a story published on Forbes.com that was written by David Blackmon, an independent energy analyst and consultant.

In my opinion, he tries to play down China's footprint in the oil and gas industry in Texas.

Blackmon does a good job listing the China deals and mentions the $1.3 billion purchase, but makes the point that it was during the "last" bust (as if it doesn't count).

He also mentions the 2010 Chesapeake Energy $2.2 billion deal where "the Chinese National Oil Company (CNOOC) purchased a non-oper-

218. CNN Business, Chinese company to buy Texas oil fields in $1.3 billion deal, Oct. 26, 2015, by Sophia Yan, https://money.cnn.com/2015/10/26/news/companies/china-texas-oilfields/index.html.

219. Fox Business News, Texas fears losing oil-rich lands in Chinese takeover of weakened energy companies, May 16, 2020, by Jonathan Garber, https://www.foxbusiness.com/markets/texas-oil-rich-lands-chinese-takeover-weakened-crude-producers.

ating 33% working interest in in Chesapeake's Eagle Ford Shale assets … CNOOC has also acquired partnership interests in two major Gulf of Mexico developments, with Shell and Hess Corp., respectively."[220]

Then he says that Chinese firms have been buying up U.S. assets for the past twenty-five years or so since China's government has been liberalizing its economy and that oil and gas are only a small part of its purchases. He makes it clear that it has been going on; they do so in countries around the world, and it is no secret.

Maybe it is not a secret, but does this make it right to sell U.S. assets to a communist nation, especially where national security is at risk?

## Thinking Realistically About Foreign Investment

I'm not saying that investment from all foreign entities is bad, but I believe boundaries must be set; otherwise, little by little, our country can be open for takeover. I fear we may be there already.

To establish my point, the following comments were made by Wayne Christian, commissioner of the Texas Railroad Commission, in the *Fox Business News* article I mentioned earlier. It sums up everything I have been saying about the Chinese takeover of the U.S. institutions:

"I believe it's a national security concern to allow unfriendly foreign countries to come in and buy land and oil in Texas and the United States… . The federal government should watch very carefully and raise their standards on who can buy," Christian said. "I don't want to wind up five years from now with, all of a sudden, some foreign country shutting down production in Texas because they own it, and prefer buying from their own reserves overseas," Christian said.[221]

---

220. Forbes.com, "No, China Is Not Buying The Permian Basin," David Blackmon, May 2020, https://www.forbes.com/sites/davidblackmon/2020/05/21/no-china-is-not-buying-the-permian-basin/?sh=6e1788629f18.

221. Fox Business News, "Texas fears losing oil-rich lands in Chinese takeover of weakened energy companies," May 16, 2020, by Jonathan Garber, https://www.foxbusiness.com/markets/texas-oil-rich-lands-chinese-takeover-weakened-crude-producers.

A foreign country does not necessarily have to march in with their military to take over. They can buy up land, real estate, politicians, businesses, and infiltrate educational institutions, culture, media, and government and stealthily whittle away at American influence and replace it with their own until our society is unrecognizable.

CHAPTER 10

# A Spiritual Solution for the Nation of Death

In this book, I've touched on the evil that is taking place in every area of our society and throughout the world. The spiritual battle we are currently experiencing in the physical realm can be overwhelming.

Some days I wonder if anything I've been trying to do is making a difference. Should I keep doing radio shows? Should I keep the radio channels on the air? Is it too late to do anything, or are we even supposed to do anything?

I believe the answer is *yes*.

Moral decay, government corruption, corporate fascism, failing healthcare and education systems, a compromised media, environmental degradation and manipulation, violence, rising crime—it seems hopeless.

Of all the strife, and particularly since the pandemic, I believe God took this evil and is waking up more and more people every day. He is putting it on their hearts to do things they thought they'd never do.

Some people have become political activists, or even started to pay attention to local politics; some are running for political office; some have become authors, speakers, broadcasters, podcasters, radio show hosts; and some are making videos to spread truth.

Some people relocated; some sold their homes; some changed jobs; and some have come to realize that instead of putting their families second to their jobs, they are reorganizing their priorities. Maybe some have even turned their lives over to Jesus Christ. Some good has come out of the bad.

So what can we do when all seems hopeless?

Many Christians do not know the power they have through the Spirit of God to combat this fear-filled, always-on-high-alert reality that is created by the globalists through the propaganda media tool.

Paul McGuire discusses the narrative of hopelessness the media pushes out 24 hours, 7 days a week and the fact that when we surrender to it, we are giving up our power, and it can become our reality. He says that through Jesus Christ, we have the power to break through what he calls the Matrix. McGuire explains: "Completely forget about religion and just think about the words of Christ when He said, 'You shall know the truth and the truth will set you free.' He was giving you a major clue on how to become free of the Matrix."[222]

On a personal note, my way of trying to break free from the hopelessness is by shutting off almost all media when things feel dark. During Covid, I would not watch the news because I believe that newscasters were programming people with the repetitive images of the spike protein, daily death counts, and dramatic music playing in the background to keep people in a constant state of fear.

When you are a believer in Jesus Christ, you don't have to live in constant fear because you know He is in control.

McGuire sums it up perfectly in this statement about what he says is the "power from on high," that supernatural power we receive through the Holy Spirit. "This is what the Bible calls receiving 'power from on high.'

222. Paul McGuire, *Mass Awakening*, (M House Publishers, Los Angeles, CA, 2015), p. 130.

The holographic reality we live in is artificial and it is based on lies and illusions, still when you access power from on high you have the ability to use that power to reconfigure reality."[223]

We have to keep in mind this fact—that we are a creation of the one and only true Creator God of the universe and we are saved through our belief in Jesus Christ. Once we accept this and truly act on it, we can be sure that through the Holy Spirit, we can fight anything earthly that comes our way.

## The Power of the Holy Spirit

One night I was attending a Christian class; we were covering a lesson that taught the power of the Holy Spirit and prayer and how it could transform many areas of life. When we think of solving life problems, we think of using human-based techniques and strategies.

This lesson was eye-opening because it focused specifically on using your words, speaking to the Holy Spirit aloud, and using the power from our almighty God to step through specific life concerns.

The lesson made me realize that many Christians have the power available to them in all areas of life, but they don't know it, so they don't use it.

So why don't Christians think about the power they have through the Word, as children of the true almighty God?

The power has been bestowed on them, but it sits on a shelf and goes unused. Meanwhile society is imploding around us. Pastors won't speak out; therefore, their flocks don't speak out. If we are not supposed to speak out, why are we here? If we are supposed to be the light, why are we hiding the light and in many cases living in fear like those that don't believe in God?

That night I realized this and shared my thoughts with the group. I

---

223. Ibid., p. 142.

told them that it seems like witches and warlocks, Satan worshipers and the like, totally believe in the power of their spoken words. This was why they cast spells and speak curses into existence, because they know they have the demonic power and authority from dark forces. They certainly don't seem to doubt it. And it seems there is something important about speaking words aloud.

So this led me to think about the etymology of the word *word*, and then of course the Word relative to God's Word.

Remember, we are made in the image of God. In the book of Genesis in the Bible, He spoke everything into existence with the authority of his Word. McGuire illustrates this in his book, *Power From on High*, he explains how the power of God's spoken words, both verbal and auditory components, are activated in a physical/scientific and spiritual sense across dimensions:

> First we have the verbal command of God, who as the Supreme Being has the power to speak or command anything into existence. The verbal or auditory command of God emanates from God who lives in another dimension beyond space and time. God's words create sound waves or specific electromagnetic frequencies which create the light ... we have a minimum of two dimensions in operation here. First, the sound waves coming from God who exists beyond space and time and then the creation of the light in the physical dimension.[224]

As I mentioned earlier, witches speak their evil spells and incantations into the air because they understand their power, while most Christians sit quietly in the corner and pray silently.

I am in no way saying that quietly praying alone is wrong, but great power is available to us through the Holy Spirit if we use it, speak it boldly, and speak loudly against evil.

---

224. Paul McGuire, *Power From on High*, (M House Publishers, Los Angeles, CA, 2022), p. 365.

## Putting on the Whole Armor of God

In the Bible, the apostle Paul teaches people how to equip themselves against the evils experienced on earth through spiritual warfare by putting on the *whole* armor of God. I believe it is time we wake up and use the *full armor of God* in these days, as revealed in Ephesians 6:10-20:

> Finally, my brethren, be strong in the Lord, and in the power of his might. *Put on the whole armor of God*, that ye may be able to stand against the wiles of the devil. For we wrestle not against flesh and blood, but against principalities, against powers, against the rulers of the darkness of this world, against spiritual wickedness in high places. Wherefore take unto you the whole armor of God, that ye may be able to withstand in the evil day, and having done all, to stand.
>
> Stand therefore, *having your loins girt about with truth*, and having on the *breastplate of righteousness*; And your *feet shod with the preparation of the gospel of peace*; Above all, taking the *shield of faith*, wherewith ye shall be able to quench all the fiery darts of the wicked. And take the *helmet of salvation*, and *the sword of the Spirit,* which is the word of God: *Praying always with all prayer and supplication in the Spirit*, and watching thereunto with all perseverance and supplication for all saints; And for me, that utterance may be given unto me, that I may open my mouth boldly, to make known the mystery of the gospel, For which I am an ambassador in bonds: that therein I may speak boldly, as I ought to speak.

McGuire reveals the importance of the spiritual tools the apostle Paul spoke about to help us in the spiritual battle we find ourselves in—we can be equipped for the battle in *both* the spiritual and physical realms.

"The full armor of God given to believers in Christ, for the purpose of spiritual warfare in the dimension of the invisible realm or spiritual world but simultaneously is a peaceful weapon in the dimension of the physical realm."[225]

Verse 10 warns and prepares us to, "be strong in the Lord and in his mighty power" because we are fighting a spiritual battle in a physical realm, and the only way we can win the battle is through the power of the Lord.

Verse 11 tells us that we need the whole armor to stand against the evil one, all of the tools of the Lord, backed by His power, "Put on the whole armor of God that ye may be able to stand against the wiles of the devil … "—in other words, physical tools would never be enough to keep back the powers of darkness.

Verse 12 tells us that while we think we are fighting earthly evils, such as tyrannical governments, murderers, slavery, drug overdoses, sexual perversion, technocrats, United Nations, and the like, it is really the wicked evil rulers of wickedness from the spiritual realm that we are fighting against.

McGuire explains each piece of armor in Ephesians 6:

*Gird your waist with truth*—gird yourself with the truth of God's Word, meaning standing in truth.

*Breastplate of righteousness*—protective armor composed of righteousness, not in the sense of good deeds, but in the righteousness of God.

*Feet shod in the gospel of peace*—being ready to share your faith in Jesus Christ at all times.

*Shield of faith*—taking the shield of faith to quench all the fiery darts of the wicked one.

*Helmet of salvation*—having the confidence of your salvation through faith in Christ.

*Sword of the Spirit*, which is the Word of God—when you use the Word of God by speaking it, reading it, using it in the form of a command, or

---

225. Paul McGuire, *Power From on High*, (M House Publishers, Los Angeles, CA, 2022), p. 365.

"binding or loosing" by invoking the authority in Christ, you are applying the Word of God in multiple dimensions.

*Praying in the Spirit*—you pray in the Spirit always with all prayer and supplication ... simply mouthing hollow and repetitive words out of tradition will produce nothing.[226]

And notice after prayer in verses 19 and 20, "And for me, that utterance may be given unto me, that I may open my mouth boldly... ." These verses specifically say that we should speak boldly.

Verse 19 does not say utterance as in a quiet manner, but says, "that I may open my mouth boldly... ." This does not mean timidly, but I would describe it as aloud, at a minimum.

McGuire reiterates this point when he speaks specifically about the sword of the Spirit, which is the Word of God, "When you use the Word of God by speaking it, reading it, using it in the form of a command, or 'binding and losing,' by invoking your authority in Christ, you are applying the Word of God in multiple dimensions."[227]

This would substantiate the reason for speaking words aloud. The power of the spoken word must go in both the physical and spiritual dimensions. This must be why the Bible warns about what you speak with your tongue, to be cautious of what you say—because there is a power behind those words. The Bible says we will have to account for the words we speak.

Matthew 12:36: "But I say unto you, That every idle word that men shall speak, they shall give account thereof in the day of judgment."

McGuire then demonstrates how apostle Paul uses the power of the Holy Spirit in his speech—in speaking against the evil and the power it has:

"The Apostle Paul needed to be prayed for by believers, so that he

---

226. Paul McGuire, *Power from on High* (M House Publishers, Los Angeles 2022), p. 365-366.
227. Ibid., p. 366.

could speak boldly, which meant that Paul was supernaturally anointed by the Holy Spirit. When Paul spoke, the full force of the Kingdom of God and the Dunamis [*miraculous*] power of the Holy Spirit would flow into his words supernaturally. It is this kind of spiritual boldness which allowed the apostle Paul to speak with the full force of the Kingdom of heaven behind him, which caused demonic powers to flee, principalities and powers to shatter, along with his words releasing the Holy Spirit."[228]

It is incredible to me that when apostle Paul spoke, the full force of the kingdom of God was behind him through the Holy Spirit. Can you imagine the full force of God's kingdom behind your words?

"When the true Remnant Church is using the Sword of the Spirit, renewing their minds with the Word of God, and is in constant prayer to God, God will clothe the church with power from on high. The church is filled with boldness, and they are fearless."[229]

Speaking boldly versus speaking quietly or timidly, the church will speak boldly!

Again, I am *not* saying silent prayer is not needed or powerful or appropriate. I do this daily.

I am saying we are currently involved in a spiritual battle. I've included many examples. I believe Christians have a supernatural power from almighty God to fight back with bold, spoken words through the power of the Holy Spirit.

I believe it was given to us not to hide away, but to use in these days.

I am not a biblical scholar, but it strikes me that if Christians speak God's Word boldly against evil, the power of that Word activates their weapon, the sword of the Spirit.

McGuire expands on this idea: "But when they use their authority

---

228. Paul McGuire, *Power from on High* (M House Publishers, Los Angeles 2022), p. 367.
229. Ibid., p. 371.

in Jesus Christ and release the cleansing power of the Holy Spirit, the demonic powers shatter and the power of the Holy Spirit is free to drive out all hindrances to God's supernatural power."[230]

I visualize it like this. We have a direct connection to our Lord Jesus Christ through the Holy Spirit. However, the devil and his demons try to block that connection or frequency—jam the signal on earth, hoping that will interfere with our connection. Using the *Word* of God, through the Holy Spirit, allows us to remove that block and re-establish that connection.

Why would demons block that frequency? Because they know the power Christians have and yet many Christians are unaware that they have it.

I think this is why censorship, especially among Christians, is on the rise. It may be about political speech now, but I think we are also seeing more Christian speech being censored.

I believe it will get worse in the coming days, months, and years until Christ's return. I see a day in the not-so-distant future where pastors will be silenced, churches will be shut down, and the Bible will be illegal.

Do you think it can't happen here? As we move away every day from the tenets of our faith in this country, we will pay the price. Many secularists wanted God out of our schools, government, and society. This is the price we will pay. When God is out of the picture, evil and tyranny take His place in a society.

Why is there an underground church in China? Is it because they are an open society that allows people to worship as they like? No, it is a tyrannical regime that will not allow people to choose how they want to worship.

This is the reason we may be on the same trajectory one day if we don't stop it.

---

230. Ibid., p. 372.

A tyrannical government works continuously and tirelessly to cover up the truth, all truth, and to promote the lies of Satan as the only truth.

## Life Through Jesus Christ

I've ended this book with the tools of the power of the Holy Spirit and the full armor of God to fight wickedness and evil in both the physical and spiritual realms, but I believe none of this matters if you are not saved by the shed blood of Jesus Christ.

Having read this book, if you are not a believer in Jesus Christ, these final words are for you. If you feel helpless, there is hope even amid the heartache in our world. The Lord Jesus Christ offers you eternal life by accepting Him as your Savior. Although, everyone dies a physical death, not everyone has to die a spiritual death.

Jesus Christ was crucified on a cross, died, and was resurrected to pay for our sins. He offers us the gift of eternal life if we simply believe He died for ours sins and accept Him as our Savior. You do not need to join a religion or group.

"Jesus saith unto him, I am the way, the truth, and the life: no man cometh unto the Father, but by me" John 14:6.

A brief prayer like this is all it takes:

Dear Lord Jesus,

Please forgive me for my sins. I accept you into my heart and my life to save my soul—as my Savior. In Jesus' name, amen.

If you are already a believer, it is time for us as the remnant to turn away from our sin, repent, and then the Bible says, "He will heal our land."

"If my people, which are called by my name, shall humble themselves, and pray, and seek my face, and turn from their wicked ways; then will I hear from heaven, and will forgive their sin, and will heal their land" 2 Chronicles 7:14.

When you feel fearful or hopeless, remember *Psalm 91:9-14:*

If you say, 'The Lord is my refuge,' and you make the Most High your dwelling, no harm will overtake you; no disaster will come near your tent.

For he will command his angels concerning you to guard you in all your ways; they will lift you up in their hands, so that you will not strike your foot against a stone.

You will tread on the lion and the cobra; you will trample the great lion and the serpent.

"Because he loves me," says the Lord, "I will rescue him; I will protect him, for he acknowledges my name."

I hope this book has clarified events that have transpired and continue to play out in our world, and I hope that your critical thinking as a truth seeker will lead you to wade through the information we are served every day.

# About the Author

Angeline Marie is a conservative Christian who believes people should think for themselves. As a journalist and talk show host, her goal is to interview guests who have done research in their areas of interest (whether she agrees with them or not) and to disseminate that information to listeners so they can use their critical-thinking skills to make up their own minds. She believes the time is short for a free people to share ideas in a free society.

Angeline Marie has worked in various behind-the-scenes roles in radio and television—she holds a Bachelor of Science Degree in Mass Communications from Florida International University in Miami, Florida.

She's the host of *The Truth Seekers Radio Show* and is program director for the K-*Star Talk Radio Network* and *Kingdom Star Radio*, conservative talk radio news and Christian faith-based teaching Internet broadcasting networks.

https://www.truthseekersradioshow.com